WHY DOES GOD ALLOW WAR?

A GENERAL JUSTIFICATION
OF THE WAYS OF GOD

WHY DOES GOD ALLOW WAR?

A GENERAL JUSTIFICATION
OF THE WAYS OF GOD

D. MARTYN LLOYD-JONES

EVANGELICAL PRESS OF WALES

© D. M. Lloyd-Jones, 1939
First published (by Hodder and Stoughton) December 1939
Reprinted January 1940, July 1940
Second edition (by the Evangelical Press of Wales) January 1986
ISBN 1 85049 023 6

Cover photograph: A casualty in the war in the South Atlantic, 1982 (by courtesy of the BBC)

Published by the Evangelical Press of Wales
Bryntirion, Bridgend, Mid Glamorgan CF31 4DX
Printed by Graham Harcourt Printers Ltd.
Fforest-fach, Swansea, West Glamorgan

TO
MY WIFE

CONTENTS

PREFACE

THESE sermons—not essays—were delivered substantially as they appear here, and in the same order, on the five Sunday mornings of October this year, at Westminster Chapel.

They are published at the request of many friends who heard them.

The theme that unites them into one series is an approach to a general theodicy, or justification of the ways of God to men.

Different aspects of the general subject are considered in each separate sermon, so that, in a sense, each is complete in itself (as should be the case always with a sermon), and at the same time contributes to the larger idea.

The whole series claims to be nothing but an approach to this great and vast subject.

The treatment is very inadequate, and I fear that the signs of hurried preparation are but too evident.

I did not set out to write a thesis or even a number of essays. I preached the messages to the people in the hope that they might help them, and strengthen their faith, in the critical days through which we are passing.

And with the same hope I now offer them to a larger public, praying that God may be pleased to use them and to bless them.

D. M. LL.-J.

Westminster Chapel,
November, 1939.

PREFACE TO THE SECOND EDITION

WHEN these sermons were first published, the Second World War was in its very early stages. My father tells us himself why he preached on this subject and then brought the sermons out in this form—'to help [people], and strengthen their faith'. Readers may wonder why the Evangelical Press of Wales feels it right to republish them forty-six years later, when Britain is not at war and when the world seems a very different place.

Yet is it so very different? As we have re-read this little book, we have been amazed at its relevance to the society in which we find ourselves. Some of the detailed circumstances are different, of course, but the fundamental problems are unchanged, and so are the great Biblical principles which we are exhorted to apply to these problems.

We, too, need help to face 'the critical days through which we are passing'.

But above all, this book is 'a theodicy, or justification of the ways of God to men'. In the third sermon we read, '. . . one of the problems that perplexes many minds at the present time . . . is the difficulty of reconciling the world in which we live, and especially what is taking place in it, with our belief in God, and especially with certain fundamentals in that belief'. This is the problem to which these sermons are addressed, and at a time like this, when there is uncertainty and confusion on all sides, in the world and in the church, it is our hope and prayer that this book will once more be used to point us to 'the depth of the riches both of the wisdom and the knowledge of God'.

ELIZABETH CATHERWOOD

June 1985

I

MAN IN THE PRESENCE OF GOD

MAN IN THE PRESENCE OF GOD

I TIMOTHY ii. 8

" I will therefore that men pray everywhere, lifting up holy hands, without wrath and doubting."

OF all the activities in which the Christian engages, and which are part of the Christian life, there is surely none which causes so much perplexity, and raises so many problems, as the activity which we call prayer. This is true at all times. But it is especially true during a time of difficulty and crisis such as a war. That was very true during the 1914-18 war, and it is certain to become one of the pressing and urgent problems as this present war proceeds. Indeed, already, it is the problem that troubles many a mind, and causes many to ask why it is that God did not hearken unto the prayers that have been offered since the crisis of September, 1938, and prevent the outbreak of this present war. It is one of the first questions, therefore, that should engage our attention.

In a time of stress and difficulty men and women turn instinctively to prayer. They are conscious of the fact that their fate, and the fate of those who are dear to them, is in the hands of powers greater than themselves. They feel that they cannot control events and circumstances as they believe they can in normal times, so they turn to God. Most people think of God and remember the possibilities of prayer when they are in desperate need, however little and however infrequently their mind may be turned in that direction at other times. They need something, and they need it urgently, so they turn to God and plead with Him to grant their request. They expect, and they wait. They are more actively engaged in a religious sense than they have ever been before. They may or may not have been formally religious, and they may have expected little from religion. But now they pin their faith to it and expect great things. And all in terms of prayer. Thus it comes to pass that there is always much talk and writing concerning this matter during a time of crisis. That alone should make us consider this question. But there are two further practical considerations that compel us to do so.

There is no aspect of the Christian life, I sometimes think, concerning which there is so much loose thinking and writing and speaking. That is largely due to the fact that those who approach it do so in the way we have indicated. They rush into prayer impelled by their need, without any real thought or study concerning the nature of prayer. And often they are encouraged to do so by teaching which seems to suggest that all they have to do is to pray, and all will be well. Thus high hopes are raised and great expectations are encouraged, and all ideas as to any conditions which have to be observed are entirely ignored. All this of necessity leads to trouble. The prayer is not answered in the way that the suppliant desired ; indeed, events may take an entirely contrary course. And, at once, the persons concerned are not only cast into a state of doubt and perplexity, but often into a condition of active criticism of God, leading finally to a loss of faith. This happened to large numbers of people during the 1914-18 war. They had prayed for the safety of their sons or for some other particular matter. The request was not granted, as they thought, and the result was that they lost their faith, and, nursing this grievance against God, they have ceased to be interested at all in religion. It is probably the experience of most pastors that they have had to deal with questions concerning the nature of prayer, and the problems that arise as the result of disappointment in connection with the matter, more frequently than with any other single question. There are other general questions which are raised by a calamity such as a war, with which we hope to deal subsequently. But the problem of prayer must come first, because it is so frequently the practical question that gives rise to so many of the other questionings. The time for us to think and to prepare is at the commencement, while there is still a certain amount of freedom and of leisure.

When feelings are hurt and susceptibilities wounded, it is difficult to do anything.

Before we come to the actual exposition of our text, it is well that we should consider certain of the commoner errors with respect to this whole question of prayer.

One of the commonest causes of difficulty, and of disappointment, is that far too frequently we approach this matter solely in terms of answers to prayer. Prayer is regarded as a mechanism which is designed to produce certain results. We need something, and we believe that all we have to do is to ask for it and that God will grant us it. We do not stop to think of how we are to approach God, and whether we have any right to do so. The idea of worshipping God and of adoring Him does not arise at all. We do not consider our respective positions or remind ourselves that He is " the high and lofty One that inhabiteth eternity " and that we are altogether sinful—our very goodness and righteousness being but " filthy rags " in His presence. The thought of listening to God and of waiting in His presence does not occur to us at all. God is but some agency to whom we can turn just when we desire to do so, and whose main function is to grant our requests. When we compare our prayers with those which we find recorded in the Bible from the lips of Moses, Daniel, Isaiah and the Apostles, and especially when we observe the order and place given to actual petitions in the model prayer taught to the disciples by our

Lord, is it not clear that we tend to leave out what is most important, and primary, and concentrate only on petitions and the gratification of our personal, selfish desires ? This is why, of course, the prayer life of so many is fitful and spasmodic in normal times, and becomes urgent and regular only in a time of desperate need.

Closely allied to this is another tendency, namely, to think overmuch in terms of what God ought to do. We have seen already that we fail to stop to consider the nature of God in the matter of our access to Him. And in the same way we fail to consider His nature and His infinite wisdom before we make up our minds as to what God ought to do. We do not hesitate to assume that what we think is right must of necessity be right, and that therefore God ought to grant us our requests in the precise form in which we present them. Alas ! how infrequently do we pause to consider what God's will may chance to be with respect to any matter. How often do we try to contemplate the various possibilities, and to envisage what may be God's will in any given situation ? How often do we seek by prayer to discover and to know the will of God ? Instead of asking Him to do His will, instead of turning to Him and saying :

> "Thy way, not mine, O Lord,
> However dark it be,"

we simply ask Him to do our will and to carry out our desires. Instead of humbling ourselves before

Him, and asking Him to reveal His will to us, we often come near to commanding God, and to dictating to Him what He should do. It is because we have already settled in our minds what must come to pass that we are so filled with chagrin, and so ready to doubt the goodness of God, when it fails to take place. This is true not only of our personal prayers, but also of our prayers with respect to our country, and perhaps our prayers with respect to the condition of the world at large.

Another very common source of trouble is to be found in the way in which we tend to draw general and sweeping conclusions from reports of answered prayers of which we read in the Bible, or elsewhere in the literature of the Church. The trouble is, that we concentrate all our attention on one aspect of the matter only, and entirely ignore the other which emphasises the conditions that must be observed in all such cases. We read of a man like George Müller or of some other Christian saint. We observe that all he had to do, apparently, was to make his request known unto God. He prayed, he made certain requests, and they were answered. There seemed to be no limit whatsoever to God's readiness to give and to respond. The prayer was offered, the answer came. We jump to the conclusion, therefore, that we have nothing to do but to pray and to make our request known to God. And when we do not receive the precise answer desired we are vexed, and hurt, and begin to doubt God. The whole trouble, of course, is entirely due to the fact that we have failed to observe the conditions. We have not noted the difference between the life lived by Müller and our lives. We have entirely missed the fact that he felt that he was called of God to exercise this particular ministry of prayer and faith, and that he knew it to be his main mission in life to tell forth the glory and the grace of God in that particular way. We have not noticed that the actual answers, and the receiving of the precise replies, were secondary matters to Müller, and that his primary concern was always, ever, the glory of God. Indeed, we may not have troubled even to notice the struggles through which he passed, and the rigid discipline which he imposed upon himself. And what is true of Müller is true of all others who have received such striking answers to their prayers. We desire to receive all the blessings which saints have received ; but we forget that they were saints. We ask, why does God not answer my prayer as He answered that man's prayer ? We *should* ask, why is it that I have not lived the type of life which that man has lived ? But in addition, as I have hinted, there is such a thing as a special calling to a ministry of intercession. Among " the diversities of gifts " which are dispensed by the Holy Spirit, St. Paul mentions " the gift of faith "—surely this special faith which manifests itself through the medium of prayer ? Were we but to realise these things, I fear we should often discover that in many of our requests we have been guilty of presumption.

One other matter to which we must refer, is the failure to discriminate between true answers to prayer and circumstances which may simulate answers to prayer. This is a very difficult subject and one concerning which we need to speak with caution. And yet it must be faced, were it merely for the reason that those who are often most guilty at this point are amongst the most spiritual of religious people, and are most concerned to tell forth the wonders of God's grace to others. This is most natural. They desire to offer to others living and actual proofs of God's direct intervention in human affairs, they long to display unmistakable tokens of His love. They are ever always on the look-out for instances and examples of this. How easy, therefore, to fail to discriminate as they ought ! And yet the New Testament in its teaching exhorts and urges us to do so. It tells us to " prove all things " and only to " hold fast " to " that which is good." It tells us that there are evil forces and powers at work in this world which are so clever, and so powerful, and so subtle in their attempts to imitate the works of God that they succeed almost in deceiving " the very elect " (Matthew xxiv. 24). Signs and wonders must be examined, and must be sifted, lest in our zeal we may at times attribute to God what is in reality the work of the devil. But, to deal with this matter on a more practical plane, is there not a danger at times of our confusing between mere coincidence and answers to prayer ? Then there are the strange

22

phenomena of telepathy and mind-transference and that whole realm which we are only just beginning to explore. It may be argued that God guides the thought of one person to another. Whether He does so or not, that is not what the Bible means by answered prayer. Neither is it what has always been accepted as the true view of this matter, which teaches that God takes action, and not merely that He directs our activities. Then there is the whole question of psychic phenomena and the problem of spiritism or " spiritualism." It is idle to deny certain well-attested phenomena, but it is vital that we should realise the nature of the agencies that produce the phenomena, and that we should be able to discriminate between the manifestations of evil spirits and the gracious working of the Holy Spirit. I have not even mentioned the power of suggestion, and the importance of an accurate medical diagnosis in reported instances of cures as an answer to prayer.

The whole subject is involved and difficult, and, to many, it may savour of unbelief that such questions should be raised at all. And yet, in the light of New Testament teaching, they are vital. Jewish exorcists and the purveyors of the art of black magic could do extraordinary things. Jannes and Jambres could enter into competition with Moses up to a point. Nothing tends to bring the gospel more into disrepute than extravagant claims, or claims which can be dismissed on natural or other grounds. I would not hesitate to say that we should be careful

23

to attribute to the direct intervention of God only that which we have entirely failed to account for by any other hypothesis. Failure to do this will inevitably lead, eventually, to muddled thinking, which in its turn will lead to disappointment and sorrow.

These, then, are the common sources of error and of trouble. We have considered them at such length, on the principle that the exposure of the nature of a trouble is more than fifty per cent of its cure. Positive instructions alone are not sufficient. But, having considered the causes of the trouble, we see clearly that one great principle emerges. And that is, that nothing is of such vital importance in connection with this whole matter of prayer as the question of the right approach. It is because we are wrong here that we are wrong everywhere. We blame God, and ask our questions. The real trouble is that we have not faced ourselves. If only we did so, half our questions would never be asked at all ; or at any rate we would be able to answer them ourselves.

Now our text deals with this very question of the approach. That is why it is so important, at such a time as this, that we should study it carefully and observe its teaching. Once we discover how to pray, how to approach the whole matter of prayer, the question of what to pray for will more or less look after itself, and the vexed problem of answers to prayer will be already solved. What I say to God in prayer is entirely subordinate to the way in which I approach God. What I am and what I have done before I begin to speak to God, are of much greater importance than my actual words. I am to concentrate, not on my prayers or the answers which I desire, first and foremost, but on myself, and on my right to pray at all. How are we to pray ? What right have we to pray ? St. Paul's answer is, " I will therefore that men pray everywhere lifting up holy hands, without wrath and doubting (or disputing)." There we have the conditions which govern the activity called prayer which we must look at briefly.

I. The first condition is that we are to lift up " *holy hands.*" We are not now concerned about the question of posture in prayer, nor to indicate that the Jews generally stood and held up their hands to God when they prayed. We shall not tarry with the fact that it was a Jewish custom to wash their hands before they took part in an act of worship. That was merely the external symbol used to emphasise the principle that the apostle is anxious to stress. The clean hands, the " holy hands," are indicative of, and represent, a holy character. That must ever be the first question in any approach to God. " Without holiness no man shall see the Lord." " God is of purer eyes than to behold evil," and cannot " look on iniquity." There is nothing which is so utterly contrary to the whole teaching of the Bible as the assumption that anyone, and at any time, without any conditions whatsoever, may approach God in prayer. Indeed, the first effect of sin, and the main result of the Fall, was

to break the communion that obtained between
God and man. Man, by sin, has forfeited his right
to approach God, and, indeed, were he left to
himself he never would approach God. But God
in His wondrous grace has made a way for man
to approach Him. That is the explanation of all
the teaching concerning offerings and sacrifices in
the Old Testament, as it is also the explanation of
the ceremonial of the tabernacle and the temple
and the Aaronic priesthood. Without these things
men could not approach God. We can commune
with Him only in this way and according to His
dictates. There is no access otherwise. But, above
and beyond all that we find in the Old Testament,
the whole meaning of the coming, and of the life
and death, resurrection and ascension, of our Blessed Lord is that they provide us with "a new and
living way" into the very presence of God. " I
am the way, the truth, and the life. No man
cometh unto the Father, but by Me." Obviously,
therefore, the first matter we have to consider
when we approach God in prayer is our own sin.
The first question must be, how can I approach
God ? What right have I to do so ? To the
Christian, the answer comes at once that " the
blood of Jesus Christ " is an atonement for our
sin, and cleanses us from it, and enables us to
approach God. But that does not mean, that
because we have believed in Christ, we can therefore live as we please and still find the way open
to God. Because we still sin, and are sinful, we

26

need to repent and ask for forgiveness anew. And repentance is not merely sorrow for sin, it is not mere remorse. It is a godly sorrow which includes the element of hatred of sin, and a determination to forsake sin and to live a holy life. In other words, this realisation of the need of cleansing, and this determination to keep " our hands " holy, are essential to our approach to God, and obviously therefore take priority over any question relative to answers to our prayer.

This is frequently emphasised in the Bible. You remember how the Psalmist puts it ? " If I regard iniquity in my heart the Lord will not hear me " (Psalm lxvi. 18). He means, that if he harbours sin in his heart, and refuses to be done with that sin, he really has no right to expect God to listen to his prayer. If his own heart condemns him, He who searches the heart and tries the spirit is certain to do so. But take another illustration. Do you remember that significant word spoken by God in Jeremiah xv. 1 ? Jeremiah was praying for his people, and this is what God said to him, "Though Moses and Samuel stood before Me, yet My mind could not be toward this people : cast them out of my sight, and let them go forth." Why Moses and Samuel ? Because they were holy men. It is as if God said to Jeremiah, " Even though the best men who have ever stood before Me pleaded for this people, I could not grant their request." There is a similar word in Ezekiel xiv. 14, where we read "Though these three men,

27

Noah, Daniel and Job were in it, they should deliver but their own souls by their righteousness, saith the Lord God." Again the explanation is the same. There is a beautiful illustration of the same point in the account of the healing of the blind man in the ninth chapter of John's Gospel. The healed man was being examined and questioned by the Pharisees, and they were trying to get him to say that Jesus could not have healed him because He was " a sinner." The man replies, " Now we know that God heareth not sinners, but if any man be a worshipper of God, and doeth His will, him He heareth." Still the same emphasis, still the same stress on the vital importance of " holy hands " if we expect our prayers to be answered. And, then, we remember the well-known word of James, " the effectual, fervent prayer of a righteous man availeth much." Fervency of spirit, and a deep desire, are not enough. It is " the righteous man " who has a right to expect the results he desires. The promises of God are never without conditions. God has not promised to grant us all our requests unconditionally ; and the first condition is ever this one of the " holy hands." It is only as we seek to conform our lives to His pattern, and determine to live according to His holy will, that we are really entitled to pray to God at all, and to bring our petitions to His throne. Are you still tempted to ask questions about God, and as to why He has not answered your prayer ?

28

II. The second condition is *" without wrath."*
It is most important that we should realise the
exact meaning of this word " wrath." It does not
mean what is usually suggested to us by the
common usage of that word. It does not mean
so much anger, or the expression or manifestation
of anger, as an unloving disposition—not a violent
outburst of temper, but rather a " settled condition
of ill-will and resentment." Here, the emphasis is
not upon the way in which a man regards God, and
approaches Him, but on the way in which he
approaches and regards his fellow-men, his neigh-
bours. Added to this, perhaps, is the whole question
of a man's spirit—not only his actions, but also his
outlook and his attitude towards others, and
towards life. How vitally important this is ! And
how tragically we all tend to fail at this point.
Often there is a feeling of resentment in our hearts
even against God while we are actually praying to
Him. We feel that we have a real grudge and a
genuine complaint. We feel that we have been
wronged. And yet we feel that we are dependent
upon God, so we ask Him for favours. We feel
that He is against us, that He is not fair to us,
and yet, in that state and condition we ask Him
to bless us, and we expect Him to do so. God
says of the Children of Israel, " this people honoureth
me with their lips but their heart is far from me."

This same spirit also shows itself in our attitude
towards our fellows. It may be a feeling of bitter-
ress, or envy, or malice, in our heart, or a refusal

to forgive them for some wrong, real or imaginary, that they have done us. And yet, though that is our attitude towards them, we expect God to forgive us and to grant us the desired answers to our petitions. Here, again, we are utterly and entirely condemned by the teaching of the New Testament. You remember the words of our Lord in the Sermon on the Mount ? " Therefore if thou bring thy gift to the altar, and there rememberest that thy brother hath ought against thee : leave there thy gift before the altar and go thy way ; first be reconciled to thy brother, and then come and offer thy gift." Again, in the Lord's Prayer we are taught to ask that God may forgive us our trespasses " as we forgive them that trespass against us." And then there is that parable recorded in the Gospel of Matthew (xviii. 23–35), where our Lord, describing the wicked servant who, having received forgiveness himself, refused to forgive the servant who owed him a debt, sums up His teaching by saying, " so likewise shall my Heavenly Father do also unto you if ye from your hearts forgive not every one his brother their trespasses." It is a terrifying thought, but it does seem to be perfectly clear and evident that those who take up an aggrieved attitude towards God and the whole world, when things go wrong with them and against them, and their prayers do not seem to be answered, were never really in a position to pray to God at all. They even refuse to forgive God (terrible, blasphemous thought !) ; and yet they are

30

the first to complain about unanswered prayer. " Without wrath." The spirit that alone entitles us to expect God to hearken to our prayers and petitions, is that which is described so perfectly and in such detail in the thirteenth chapter of the First Epistle to the Corinthians. If we are slaves, we must not have a feeling of wrath towards kings and all who sit in authority ; and if we have enemies, we must not hate them, but love them. The rule is " love your enemies, bless them that curse you, do good to them that hate you, and pray for them which despitefully use you, and persecute you." " Without wrath."

III. The third condition is described as " *without doubting*," or, if you prefer it, " without disputing." The reference is not to disputing with others, but to disputing with oneself. It denotes a state of wavering and uncertainty, or, perhaps, even a state of actual intellectual rebellion. The doubt may express itself in many different ways. It may be doubt with respect to the very being of God ; doubt, to use the words of the author of the Epistle to the Hebrews, as to whether " God is." It is remarkable to note how many people pray without even settling this first and fundamental prerequisite to prayer and its possibilities. Others, while being quite clear on this matter, are in a state of doubt with regard to the goodness of God, and of God's readiness and willingness to hearken to our prayers. This is a matter with which we hope to deal at greater length in subsequent considerations of this

31

general question of God's ways towards men. But, here, we must indicate that it is surely obvious, if we but take the trouble to think for a moment, that such a state and condition on our part render our prayers useless. And then there is often doubt with respect to what we may call the power or the possibility of prayer, as to whether anything can happen or ever does happen, in a word, whether there is any point in our praying at all.

As a result of these doubts, whether only one of them, or all of them together, it often comes to pass that prayer is nothing but some desperate adventure or doubtful experiment in which we engage. We find ourselves in a difficult position, or face to face with some dire need. We know not what to do, or where to turn. Then we remember that we have heard about someone who prayed to God, and had a marvellous answer. So we decide to pray, to try the experiment, in order to see whether it will succeed with us also. We have not thought the matter out thoroughly, we have not stopped to consider all the conditions to which we have referred ; we more or less " cry out in the dark," on the possible chance that it may succeed, and we may be delivered. In that state of doubt and scepticism, and, indeed, at times, of actual disbelief, men often pray to God ; and when their prayers are not answered, and their desires are not satisfied, they grumble and complain, pronounce religion to be useless, and take umbrage against God. Unless we observe this third condition, prayer is useless. We must approach God believing "that He is, and that He is a rewarder of them that diligently seek Him." Prayer is not meant to be the doubtful experiment that may lead to faith and belief; it is rather the expression, and the outcome, of a faith that not only believes in God, but is also prepared to trust its all to Him and to His holy will. To pray to God in order to discover whether prayer works or not is an insult to God. And there can be but one outcome to such an experiment. The men whose prayers have been answered have always been those who knew God, those who have trusted Him most thoroughly, those who have been most ready to say at all times and in all circumstances " Thy will be done," assured as they were of His holy and loving purpose. There must be no doubt, no disputing, no desperate experiments, but rather a calm and unhurried resting upon, and in, God and His perfect will.

These, then, are the conditions. Do you not agree, as you consider them, that the surprising thing is not that God at times does not answer our prayers as we desire Him to do, but rather that He should ever hearken unto us at all, and grant us any of our requests ? Let us, then, resolve to put these principles into practice while there is still time. The acute crisis may come at any moment, and we may feel the need of prayer. Let us cleanse our hands, purify our spirits, and be established in our faith. And then, in the hour of our greatest crisis, we shall not be making a doubtful experiment, but rather turning to One of Whom we can say with St. Paul, " I know Whom I have believed, and am persuaded that He is able to keep that which I have committed unto Him against that day." The answer may not always be what we had desired, but we shall be enabled to see that ultimately it was that which was best for our souls. And, in any case, we shall have learned to be more concerned about the glory of God than the gratification of our own desires.

II

FACING THE UNEXPECTED

FACING THE UNEXPECTED

JUDGES xiii. 22 AND 23

" And Manoah said unto his wife, We shall surely die, because we have seen God. But his wife said unto him, If the Lord were pleased to kill us, he would not have received a burnt offering and a meat offering at our hands, neither would he have shewed us all these things, nor would as at this time have told us such things as these."

THESE words are the simple yet profound record of how the father and mother of Samson reacted to the same set of difficult and critical circumstances in which they suddenly found themselves. But they are not simply a record, they are at the same time a judgment. The record of what these two people did and said tells us all about them, passes judgment upon them. The real meaning of the word crisis is judgment, and thus it comes to pass that any crisis through which we may be passing becomes incidentally a time of testing for us. And as we see so clearly in this old anecdote, the crisis, among many other things that it does, brings out very definitely two vitally important things with respect to us.

For one thing, it shows exactly and precisely what kind of person we really are. You can read the whole of this chapter prior to our text and

still not really know Manoah and his wife. Until
we arrive at these verses it is almost impossible to
assess these two persons, and to tell which of the
two is the stronger or the finer character. But
here, in these two verses, suddenly and in a flash,
we see them as they are, we get to know them
thoroughly, and the forming of an opinion and
an estimate becomes a matter of supreme ease.
Manoah's wife stands out not only by way of
contrast to her husband, but also as one of the
truly great women of the Bible.

Now that is a reminder to us of a principle which
is universally true. In normal times, when life is
pursuing the ordinary tenor of its way, we all
succeed in making a fair show. We adopt a certain
standard and a certain attitude towards life, and
there is sufficient time and leisure to enable us to
carry out the part. We observe the rules and
conform ourselves to the various standards that
are recognised. We make our professions and
protestations with respect to what we think, and
what we believe, and with regard to what we
propose to do face to face with certain hypothetical
possibilities. And thus we give to others a certain
impression of ourselves and the kind of person we
really are. I am not suggesting that the whole of
life is just one great hoax and fraud, but I am
suggesting seriously that, unconsciously, we all
tend to play a part in life, and, thereby, not only
deceive others but ourselves also. It is so easy to
live an artificial and a superficial life and to persuade

ourselves that we really are what we would like
to be. The actor is strong in all of us, and in
times like these, when the tyranny of social con-
ventions and forms has been so strong, one of the
most difficult things in life is for us to put into
practice the advice of the ancient philosopher—
" know thyself." Now if *we* find it difficult to do
this, a time of trial and of crisis invariably does
it for us. It comes to us suddenly and finds us
" off guard." There is no time to remember the
conventionalities and the customs, no opportunity
as it were of putting on the mask, we just act
instinctively. The natural, the real, and the true
come into view.

But a crisis tests us in a still deeper sense, and
especially in the matter of our professions and
protestations. The wisdom of the world reminds
us that " a friend in need is a friend indeed." It
talks about " fair-weather friends." It is what a
man does in the moment of need that really proclaims what he is, not his promises and general
sentiments expressed lavishly during a period of
tranquillity. Indeed, our Lord warned us repeatedly
against this very danger in such words as : " Not
every one that saith unto me Lord, Lord, shall
enter the kingdom of heaven, but he that doeth
the will of my Father, which is in heaven." Our
behaviour in times of need, difficulty and of crisis
really proclaims what we are ; and that is why such
times are always times of sad disappointment and
disillusionment and of strange surprises. Those

who have been loudest in their talk suddenly become silent, and those who had purposed to do so much quietly disappear.

But still more important from our standpoint, and for our immediate purpose, is the realisation that a time of crisis and of difficulty also tests and demonstrates very clearly what we really believe, and the nature of our religious faith. For, after all, merely to see the greatness of Samson's mother as a woman, and as a strong character, is to miss what is really significant in the story. The striking thing is the faith, the insight, the understanding, the firm grasp of religion which really made her what she was, and which enabled her to shame her husband and to reproach him for his weakness and his fear. The Bible is not very interested in natural greatness of character—its theme everywhere is greatness as the result of grace. The testing conditions in which Manoah and his wife found themselves revealed at once the nature and, therefore, the precise value of their profession of religion. There, again, we have another universal principle, which works itself out and manifests itself in different ways.

It may be that we have been brought up in a religious atmosphere and surrounded from our very birth by religious teaching. Being brought up in this way we had heard certain things and had become familiar with religious truths. Everyone round about us seemed to believe them, and, in time, we found ourselves repeating them and regarding ourselves as true believers in them. We never thought of examining these beliefs, still less of doubting them. We just seemed to accept everything without thinking at all deeply about them. We assumed that everything was all right and that we ourselves also were all right. We had not taken the trouble really to understand and to try to comprehend all these statements about religion. We had not troubled really to take in the teaching. As I heard a man once put it, we had taken our religion very much in the same way as we had taken our bread and butter daily from the table. And while all was well, we had gone on with our religion and its duties, assuming that we had the right and the real thing, and without suspecting any real lack or need. But suddenly, we were confronted by a difficulty, a problem, and face to face with this we found ourselves behaving and reacting almost in precisely the same way as men and women who have never laid any claim to religion whatsoever. We were equally helpless and equally hopeless. Our religion seemed to make no difference.

There is nothing which is quite so sad and so tragic in the life and experience of a minister as to find people of this type whose religion does not seem to give them anything, or to be of the slightest value to them face to face with the greatest needs and crises of life such as illness, bereavement and sorrow, disaster or threatened calamity, or a war. They had appeared to be such excellent examples of religious people. They had never been guilty of any heretical statement or of any gross violation of the moral code. They seemed in times of normality to be the ideal type of religious person. And yet, when their religion was put to the test and was needed most of all, it suddenly seemed to mean nothing and to be quite useless. Have you not known such people ?

But there are others also in this group, though not for precisely the same reason. I refer to those whose interest in religion has been mainly, and indeed almost entirely, intellectual. It cannot be said of them, as of those we have just been considering, that they have not thought at all, for they have. Their interest in religion has been their main intellectual hobby. They have read and reasoned and debated and argued about it. They are interested in it as a view of life, interested in its various propositions and positions. But all the time, their interest has been purely objective. Religion was something to talk about and to argue about, something which a man could take up and put down. It had never become a part of their inner actual experience. It had never become a part of them and of their lives. It had played no experimental and vital part in their existence. They seemed to know all about it. But here again, in the crisis, all the knowledge and the interest seem to be useless and valueless.

The classic example of this, of course, is John Wesley prior to his conversion. He, in a sense, knew all about religion, but while crossing the Atlantic, and in a terrible storm which seemed to be leading to certain death, he felt that he had nothing. He was afraid to die and afraid of everything. And what struck him was the contrast presented by the Moravian Brethren who were in the same ship. They were in comparison with Wesley ignorant men, but their religion meant something real and vital to them. It held them in the storm, and gave them peace and calmness, and indeed joy, even face to face with death. Wesley's religion appeared to be excellent. He gave all his goods to the poor, he preached in prisons, and he had crossed the Atlantic to preach to pagans in Georgia. He was a man of immense knowledge of things religious. And yet the trial revealed to him and to others the nature of his religion, and showed it to be worthless. A time of crisis, then, tests us and our religion, even as it tested Manoah and his wife.

Now the tragedy is that so many of us resemble the former rather than the latter. We are anxious to be blessed, and we look to religion for all the gifts and blessings that it has to give. Like Manoah we may be fervent in our prayers and, judged by actions and our external appearance, we may appear and, indeed, actually be, highly devout persons. While all goes well, and while our prayers are answered and all our desires appear to be gratified, we are full of praise and of thanksgiving, even as Manoah was when his request was granted. But, then, suddenly, something happens which we do not quite understand. Something takes place which is quite unexpected. The clouds gather, the sky is darkened, everything seems to go wrong. The situation is perplexing and baffling and quite the contrary of what we had expected and anticipated. Now, far too often, face to face with this we behave as Manoah did. We seem to break down altogether and to lose hope entirely. We jump to conclusions, and, almost invariably, to the worst conclusion that is possible in the given circumstances. Still worse, this " worst conclusion " to which we jump so readily is far too frequently a conclusion that is based upon the same assumption as that which led Manoah to his worst conclusion, viz. that somehow or other, God is against us, and that all we had so fondly imagined to be an expression of God's goodness and kindness was nothing but an illusion.

I say all this on the basis of the statements made by men and women when they are face to face with such crises. How ready they are to ask questions which should never be asked, questions with the implied statement that somehow God is not being fair to them, or that God is not consistent with His promises. This, surely, is the most persistent enemy of the human race, indeed the most persistent enemy of the Christian in particular. I mean this suggestion which the enemy of our souls is always so ready to insinuate into our minds and hearts that God is against us, or, at any rate, that God is not very concerned about us and our welfare. The old pagan conceptions, the old superstitious ideas cling to us most tenaciously, and are ever ready to offer themselves as explanations when we are confronted by a baffling situation. If we but grumbled at the situation our case would not be quite so bad, although then it would be the indication of a very poor and weak type of Christianity. But we tend to go further. We grumble and complain not merely at what is happening to us, but at God Himself. We ask our questions. We make our statements which, however guarded they may be, suggest strongly that we doubt Him and His goodness to us.

It is scarcely necessary to point out what is involved in such a state. And yet we must just indicate how terribly dishonouring to God it is. This is the central cause of all ills ; this is the sin of all sins, the sin of unbelief. It is not for us to compare sin with sin, but surely the Bible shows very clearly that failure in conduct, or even a moral lapse, is nothing in comparison with this sin of unbelief. For this displays an attitude which is fundamentally hostile and inimical to God, whereas the other is but a manifestation of human weakness and frailty. To doubt God and His goodness is a very much more heinous sin than to fail to obey Him or to carry out His commandments. We need say no more.

But this condition is also entirely indefensible when we consider ourselves with respect to other people. Manoah should have helped and strengthened his wife. The natural thing would have been for her to look to him. Fortunately for her, she was not dependent upon him, otherwise his collapse would have led to a still greater collapse in her case. But the facts are not always so. Within the Christian life and within the life of the Church, there are always people who look to us and who depend upon us. That is, at one and the same time, our privilege and our responsibility. When we fail, therefore, others are involved in our failure. And when we realise that there are always those entirely outside Christianity who look to Christians, and especially in times of difficulty and of stress, our failure becomes still more reprehensible.

But even from our own strictly personal standpoint this Manoah-like behaviour is thoroughly bad. It leads to a state of wretchedness and hopelessness. It means that we are unhappy and miserable, agitated and alarmed, and full of fears and evil forebodings, with all that such feelings inevitably lead to. But still more important, in that state and condition we are liable to say things, even as Manoah did, things which we will afterwards regret and deplore as long as we live.

For those reasons alone we should always be careful. But all this is negative, and we can now proceed to something positive. We need not behave as Manoah did. His wife shows us clearly how all that is to be avoided. God grant that we may learn the lesson now, so that whatever may come to meet us in the future we shall be ready and prepared, forearmed, and able to forestall the enemy who will certainly come to us with his hateful suggestion that God is either failing us, or else is definitely against us.

The teaching divides itself very naturally into two main divisions.

I. We must consider first what this woman did. And the answer is the rather startling and surprising one, that *she just thought and reasoned*. How simple ! And yet how we tend to fail at that point. The reasons for the failure are many. I note but two which I have found most frequently. The one is what we may call in general an anti-intellectual spirit with regard to religion. It does not always recognise itself as such, and it is not always aware of itself as such, but there has been a great deal of this attitude to religion during the past years. Precise thinking, and definition, and dogma have been at a serious discount. The whole emphasis has been placed upon religion as a power which can do things for us and which can make us happy. The emotional and feeling side of religion has been over-emphasised at the expense of the intellectual. Indeed, we may say that the miraculous side of, and the miraculous element in, the Christian religion has been given undue prominence. Far too often people have thought of it merely as something which gives a constant series of miraculous deliverances from all sorts and kinds of ills. The slogans of which we have heard so much

47

testify to this. The phrases most frequently used have been " Try religion " or " Try prayer," and the impression has often been given that we have but to ask God for whatever we may chance to need and we shall be satisfied. That practical side of religion has been stressed, without anything being said about conditions and about the whole scheme of salvation, and about the revelation of the nature and the purposes of God as revealed in the Bible. The type of religion that has been most popular has been that which represents itself as being " quite easy " and " quite simple," and which seems to do everything for us without demanding anything of us. Never perhaps has the distinction between the Christian religion and the various cults and psychological agencies which try to help men been more obscured and confused than during the past twenty years. The great principles, the mighty background, the intellectual and theological content of our faith have not been emphasised, and indeed, oftentimes, have been dismissed as being non-essentials. We have been so intent upon ourselves and our moods and feelings and inward states, that when we are confronted by an external problem that nevertheless affects us profoundly, we do not know how to think or where to begin.

The other reason which explains why we fail to think, as this woman did, is that in some sudden crisis we tend to be stunned and to allow ourselves to be stampeded. I am prepared to grant that this may be partly physical or nervous. But it is not entirely so. In such conditions we tend to " let go " and to let ourselves go. We abandon ourselves, and we cease to struggle and to make a positive effort. We not only lose grip of ourselves, in a sense we deliberately relax and let go. It is not merely laziness, but a manifestation of the kind of intoxicating effect that a calamity, or a shock, or a crisis always tends to have upon us. How easy it is to shout or to scream or to give way to some other impulse that is certain to arise on such occasions ! How easy to let go the reins of self-control and self-mastery.

Now this woman, the mother of Samson, stands out as a glorious example of the opposite of all that. She behaved as we should all behave. She did what we should all do in like circumstances. Seeing and observing her husband's collapse, his fear and his whimpering, and listening to his foreboding of evil and his dark prophecies and his doubtings of the goodness of God, she doesn't cry or shout, she doesn't give way to hysteria and finally collapse in a state of unconsciousness, she doesn't ask irreverent questions or utter complaints against God—she thinks, she reasons, she ponders the matter, and with magnificent logic she arrives at the only conclusion that is really valid. It may sound strange and odd to you that, in the midst of disaster and trying difficulties, the Christian religion instead of acting like a charm or a drug, and doing everything for us, and suddenly putting everything right, asks us, nay rather commands us, to think and to employ logic. But such is its teaching not only here but everywhere else in the Bible. I would summarise its instructions as follows :—

(1) Don't speak until you have considered the matter. Take yourself firmly in hand, control yourself and specially your lips. Say nothing until you have thought, and thought deeply. In the words of James " be slow to speak."

(2) Then make the positive effort and think actively. Don't merely contemplate the facts and allow certain thoughts to go on repeating themselves in your mind. Think actively. Regard it as your duty to think as you have never thought before, and as if the very character of God and His justification before men depended upon you. The enemy has attacked you, and especially in the realm of your mind. Withstand him and rout him !

(3) Start from the assumption that whatever else may be true, and however little you may understand, one thing is certain and absolute— the enemy's suggestion about God is, and must be of necessity, wrong.

(4) Then determine to consider all the facts, and not merely one fact, or certain of the facts. Manoah in a sense was quite logical. He knew that anyone who saw God must certainly die. His trouble was that he considered that fact alone without putting the other facts that were available with it, and, thereby, he arrived at a false conclusion. From one fact only he jumped to his conclusion. How

often have we all done so! Avoid that, by determining to consider other facts. Place the problem in the light of its larger context. There, then, we are shown by the action of Manoah's wife what we should do in like circumstances. We must think and reason.

But, fortunately for us, the lesson goes still further. For we are not merely told that she thought, we are given the result of her reasoning and logic.

II. We can consider, therefore, in the second place, *what this woman said*. Her conclusions are as valid to-day as when she uttered them. She simply stated in her own way, and in her own language, and in the context of the events which confronted her and her husband, what St. Paul says and argues constantly in his various epistles. Indeed, we have here a wonderful and very picturesque summary and epitome of the whole of the consolatory teaching of the New Testament. I will summarise what she says by putting it into the form of a number of propositions.

(a) The first principle is that *God is never capricious*. " If the Lord were pleased to kill us " argues the woman, " he would not have received a burnt offering and a meat offering at our hands." It appeared at the moment as if God were suddenly going to reverse everything that He had just been doing. Having smiled upon these people, it looked as if without any apparent cause or reason He was now frowning upon them, and on the point of destroying them. Circumstances often seem to give us that impression. Everything suddenly seems to go wrong and to be working in the reverse direction, and the suggestion comes to us that God is not really interested in us, and not concerned about us. His very kindness in the past and all the blessings seem to be just mocking us. And the temptation is to think that God is like certain earthly human potentates and tyrants who delight to play with their victims, and to increase their terror and their torture, by pretending at first to be kind to them. There is nothing which is so humiliating, and so nerve-racking, as to be at the mercy of, or under obligation to, a person who is unreliable, whose moods are constantly changing, and whose purposes and actions are correspondingly variable. Never for a moment does one feel safe. At any moment something may be done which is a complete reversal of all that has gone before. There is no sense of security or of peace. There is no hope as one looks to the future. Now, of one thing we can always be absolutely and definitely certain —God is not like that. And He will never behave in that manner. Whatever the appearances may be, that is not the explanation. By His very nature and being there is nothing more glorious than the eternal constancy of God. He is the Eternal, and His decrees are eternal. His goodness and His kindness are everlasting. And His dealings with the children of men are the outcome of this. His plans were made, as we are told repeatedly, " before

the foundation of the world." He loves with an
" everlasting love." He is " the father of light
with whom is no variableness neither shadow of
turning." He does not say one thing and then do
the opposite. He does not play with us and mock
us. Yea " if the Lord were pleased to kill us, He
would not have received a burnt offering and a
meat offering at our hands." He is never
capricious.

(b) The second principle is that *God is never
unjust in His dealings with us*.

Samson's mother argues very rightly, that for
God to have led her and her husband to do certain
things merely in order that He might punish and
destroy them for so doing, would be an act of sheer
injustice. And that is something which she knows
to be utterly unthinkable where God is concerned.
It is not that she understands exactly and precisely
what is happening to them, or as to what is the
exact meaning of the events which they are witness-
ing. But, whatever their meaning may be, of this
she is certain, that God is never unjust or un-
righteous. Seeing, as we do, but one aspect or one
angle or phase of a problem or a situation, we often
fail to see the righteousness or the justice of events.
But that is entirely due to our restricted field of
vision. Furthermore, our minds are warped, and
we are tarnished and perverted by sin. Our very
ideas of rightness are not true. Our selfishness
blurs our vision and poisons our understanding.
We do not even know what is ultimately the best

for ourselves, there is so much darkness mixed with our light. And thus, in our folly, we are ready to charge God with being unjust, or unfair, or un-righteous. Manoah's wife saw the utter folly and error and sin of all this. And in her own way she proclaimed " God is light and in Him is no dark-ness at all," and asked the question already asked by Abraham, " shall not the Judge of all the earth do right ? "

Beware of judging God with your feeble sense, but decide rather with this woman and with an old hymn-writer to say :

> " Whate'er my God ordains is right :
>   Holy His will abideth ;
>   I will be still whate'er He doth,
>   And follow where He guideth :
>   He is my God ;
>   Though dark my road,
>   He holds me that I shall not fall :
>   Wherefore to Him I leave it all.

> " Whate'er my God ordains is right :
>   He never will deceive me ;
>   He leads me by the proper path,
>   I know He will not leave me :
>   I take, content,
>   What He hath sent ;
>   His hand can turn my griefs away,
>   And patiently I wait His day."

(c) The third principle is that *God never contradicts Himself and His own gracious purposes.*

Listen to this woman's superb logic. "If the Lord were pleased to kill us . . . he would not have shewed us all these things nor would as at this time have told us such things as these." In effect, she turned to her husband and said, Is it conceivable that the God Who has just given us such striking tokens of His presence and His goodness is now going to destroy us? Nay, more, is it conceivable that the One Who has intervened in our lives, and has come to us to tell us that He has certain plans in store for us and certain purposes which He proposes to bring to pass in us and through us, is it conceivable that having initiated all this He is now suddenly going to end it all? I do not pretend to understand, but, to me, it is unthinkable that God should start a process and then suddenly reverse it or destroy it.

There again we have in her words what St. Paul states so frequently and so eloquently. Listen to him: "Being confident of this very thing, that he which hath begun a good work in you will perform it until the day of Jesus Christ." But the argument is still stronger, "He that spared not His own Son but delivered Him up for us all, how shall he not with him also freely give us all things?" Is God Who has already done the greater, yea, the greatest thing of all, likely to fail us in the lesser? Is the love of God, which is so great as to send His only-begotten Son to that cruel death on Calvary's Hill, likely to forsake you, having done that? You may not understand what is happening to you. It may seem to you all wrong, but trust yourself to Him. Believe when you cannot prove. Hold on to His constancy, His justice, His eternal purposes for you in Christ. Regard these as absolutes, which can never be shaken, build your case logically upon them, remain steadfast and unshaken, confident that ultimately all will be made plain and all will be well.

And in that mood, but not until you have arrived at it, *speak* to yourself and to others, and say :

> " The work which His goodness began,
>   The arm of His strength will complete ;
> His promise is Yea and Amen,
>   And never was forfeited yet.
> Things future, nor things that are now,
>   Nor all things below nor above
> Can make Him His purpose forego,
>   Or sever my soul from His love."

III

THE MYSTERY OF GOD'S WAYS

THE MYSTERY OF GOD'S WAYS

ISAIAH xlv. 15

" Verily Thou art a God that hidest Thyself, O God of Israel, the Saviour."

THIS magnificent apostrophe, this outburst of devout worship and adoration, breaks from the lips of the prophet as the result of God's revelation to him of His plans and purposes. It does not record a complaint. It is the expression, rather, of amazement and astonishment at the wonderful ways of God. Whether the prophet himself had shared the views of the people in general, and was guilty of the same lack of insight and of faith we cannot tell, but God's answer to the thoughts and murmurings of the people overwhelms him in its magnificence and grandeur.

The state of mind of the people is portrayed in vivid and striking terms in the earlier verses of the chapter. They were perplexed and baffled, nay, more, they were full of doubts and of questionings. All this, of course, as the result of the situation in which they found themselves, and because of the events that were taking place. Added to these was the announcement of the way of deliverance that God proposed and intended to employ. The facts were these. The Children of Israel, as a nation and people, were experiencing a constant series of reverses and humiliations. They knew that they were the chosen people, the special people of God, and yet they were becoming weaker and weaker, and their enemies—heathen and strangers from the commonwealth of Israel—were constantly gaining in strength. The land of Israel had been repeatedly attacked, and their armies defeated. The enemy had carried away some of their most valuable treasures, and indeed had carried away as captives a large number of the people. At the moment, it was clearly but a matter of time before Jerusalem herself should be conquered and destroyed, and the remainder of the people carried away captive to Babylon. Everything had gone wrong, and the enemy was increasingly powerful. And in the meantime God was apparently doing nothing. He had in no way hindered or restrained the arrogant enemy. God did not seem to be concerned at all. Certainly He had not intervened to deliver His people and to destroy the enemy. They were baffled and amazed, and began to ask questions. Why did God behave in this manner ? Why did God allow the enemy to flourish and to prosper ? And then certain darker questions were asked. Could God stop it ? Had He the power to do so —had He " the hands " to do so ?

All this was accentuated when the announcement was made, through the prophet, that ultimately deliverance was to come through Cyrus. That seemed to be the very last straw. Deliverance through a Gentile, and not through an Israelite and one who belonged to the seed of David? It was surely impossible. What did God mean? Was it just and righteous? Should God do such a thing? How could it be reconciled with all He had done and said in the past, and with all His promises and plans? Such was the state of the people mentally and spiritually, and such were the questions that they asked, or, rather, the statements they made.

In this mighty passage God answers the people by reminding them of His nature and His power, His knowledge and His purposes. He rebukes them, and, through the prophet, gives them a glimpse into the future into which He proposes to lead them. The prophet can no longer contain himself. Forgetting the people, and turning from them, he addresses God directly in these words of wonder and of praise—"Verily Thou art a God that hidest Thyself, O God of Israel, the Saviour."

It would be good and most instructive to consider this matter in its own precise context and setting, and to shew how it all actually worked out in the story of the Children of Israel. But, while we shall be doing that in a sense, we must concentrate on it, rather, as it applies to us, and speaks to us, face to face with the contemporary situation. It is scarcely necessary to point out that here we have a consideration of one of the problems that perplexes many minds at the present time, a problem that has also worried many for a number of years past. In a word, the problem is the difficulty of reconciling the world in which we live, and especially what is taking place in it, with our belief in God, and especially with certain fundamentals in that belief. At first, the perplexity caused by this problem expresses itself as a general statement, more or less to this effect. For years it has been evident that the forces of evil and wrong have been increasingly in the ascendancy. Materialism, godlessness, irreligion, sin and evil, vice and wrongdoing have been on the increase. The whole religious basis on which the life of the country has been founded in the past has not only been questioned, but also ridiculed and derided. The Church, from being patronised, has been dismissed. Far from being persecuted, she has just been ignored and forgotten, and her story from year to year has been one of continued decline and difficulty. The more arrogant the worldling has become, the more successful apparently has been his life. Everything seems to be on the side of evil and wrong ; all that is most hostile to God and His Church, and to the view of life denominated Christian, is rampant, and flourishing on all sides. The decline in religion and morals, and in every uplifting and ennobling view of life, has continued at an alarming and terrifying rate. The world has gone from bad to worse with evil men " waxing worse and worse," and the whole of life seems to be heading straight for the abyss. The world has more and more

62

become the very exact opposite of everything that God would desire it to be, and now that the drift to war of the past few years has actually landed us in war, all seems to be lost. The situation has become steadily more and more hopeless. Now while all this has been taking place, and is taking place, God has appeared to be strangely silent and inactive. He seems to have done nothing and has in no way intervened to arrest this process. He does not seem to be in evidence, or indeed, in existence at all. The only activity in the world appears to be the activity of evil. God seems to have been absent and altogether outside the course of events. He has done nothing, and the enemy has prevailed. Such is the statement ; and it leads inevitably to the question that is asked so frequently—Why does God allow such things to happen ? Why does He not intervene ? Why does He not restrain evil and evil-doers ? Why does He not revive His work and rescue the Church from her impotence and her shame? Why does God not hearken to the prayers of His people, and destroy evil-doers and all their ways, and restore the world to a right and to a true way of life ? How is it that He can, as it were, stand aside and do nothing, and allow everything that is worth-while and noble to be destroyed and desecrated ? Such are the forms taken by the one general question of why does God behave in this manner, and apparently allow everything that He hates to develop and to flourish ?

But the questioning never stops at that point.

Having reached so far, it seems to be carried along by an inevitable momentum to a series of further questions which are more serious and ominous. These further questions are dealt with in this passage. We must consider them individually and separately, remembering as we do so, that we are not engaged in an academic study or psychological analysis of people who lived nearly three thousand years ago, but in a study of ourselves and of the errors to which we are as prone as the Children of Israel were.

1. The first question can be put in these terms— *Is God indifferent?* Is it the truth that He does not care as to what is happening to us, and in the world? That, certainly, is the question that is implied in the whole of this passage which we are considering. The Children of Israel felt that God was neglecting them, and that He was no longer looking after them, and caring for them, as He had done formerly. They felt that He had become indifferent and unconcerned, that He had definitely turned His face away from them, and was allowing events to follow their own course. That seemed to them to be the most obvious and the most ready explanation of what was happening to them, and of God's strange silence and inactivity. How often have men come to that conclusion! How many are tending to do so at the present time! It is not that they have adopted the view propounded by the deists of old. They taught that God, having created the world, had then ceased to be actively concerned about it. God, they said, having made

the world as a watchmaker makes a watch, and having wound up the watch, was now allowing it to run on and to run out in its own way. God had finished with it in the sense of an active concern and interference. I do not know that there are many who actually hold that view to-day. The view, rather, is that, for some reason or other, God has ceased to be actively interested. They know that He has been interested in the past, through His works, even as the Israelites knew that. His silence and inactivity therefore, they argue, must denote an indifference, as if God had lost patience with the world, and, abandoning it to its fate, had turned His back upon it. The faithful pray and strive and work, and yet there seems to be no response from the side of God. How easy it is to argue from this that God is indifferent! Is it not the implication in most of the questions that are asked as to why God allows certain things to happen? And, often, the implication is more in the tone of voice than in the actual question itself. The feeling is, that if God were truly a God of love, He could not allow the righteous to suffer as they sometimes do, and the unrighteous to flourish and succeed, that He could not allow calamities and wars and all the other afflictions and tribulations that come to try us. Why does God allow it? they ask. Yea, more, how *can* He allow it? And in spite of the sufferings and the prayers of the people? Yea, as a psalmist once put it, " Will the Lord cast off for ever? and will He be favourable

65

no more ? Is His mercy clean gone for ever, doth His promise fail for evermore ? Hath God forgotten to be gracious ? Hath he in anger shut up His tender mercies ? " The charge, in the first question, is that God is indifferent.

2. But another question insinuates itself also, and partly as a possible answer to the first question. It is—*Is God impotent ? Can* He do anything ? That is the question mentioned in the last phrase of verse 9. Having asked, " Shall the clay say to him that fashioneth it, what makest thou ? " it goes on to ask " or thy work, He hath no hands ? " which Moffat translates "does what he makes tell him that he is powerless?" As if the clay could tell the potter that he lacked skill or power to mould and to make a vessel, so men query and question the power and the capacity of God to control events in the world, and to hearken to their prayers. They feel that this conclusion is inevitable. They have no doubt that if God *could* arrest evil and stem the tide of iniquity He *would* do so. His love, they argue, would insist upon that ; it is inconceivable that it would not. Therefore there can be but one conclusion. It must be that God lacks the power, that the might of evil is greater than the power of God. It must be that the world has got " out of hand," and beyond the power of God to control and to save it. Darkness and evil are perchance outside of and beyond the power of God. That is the second question.

3. But there is a third question, which arises on

account of what God proposes to do and announces
as His future action. This use of Cyrus as a de-
liverer—*does not that mean that God is inconsistent?*
How can that tally with all the past? A Gentile
to deliver Israel? One who was not of the seed
of David to be the saviour of the people? An
outsider? Why, it seems unthinkable. It would
be adding insult to injury! It would be un-
righteous on the part of God. God must not do
it, because it would be quite out of line with all
that He had said and had promised, and out of
line with all that He had done in the past. They
felt that to employ the Gentile Cyrus was something
that could never be reconciled with the holiness of
God. It appeared to them to be tantamount to
expecting good to come out of evil, that anyone
outside the commonwealth of Israel should be used
by God to bring His purposes to pass. They could
see no possible explanation. It seemed to them to
be altogether and entirely wrong. Have we not
all known something of that feeling and of that
state of mind? How can this thing which is
happening to us, we have asked, possibly be for
our good and to the glory of God? What possible
justification of God can there be for allowing us
to suffer? How can trials and tribulations con-
ceivably be a part of God's plan or scheme? Can
that which is patently wrong and evil be brought
anyhow, or by any means, within the ambit of
God's love and God's sovereign purpose with respect
to us and to mankind?

Such are the questions that are considered here, even as they are the questions that are still being asked by men. Have you asked them? What is to be said about them? What is the answer to them?

Let us consider the mighty answer of this word of Isaiah. The matter divides itself very simply into two main statements.

I. *The arrogance displayed in this attitude towards God.* This is what is emphasised in the various comparisons of man in his relationship to God, to the potsherds and the clay, and the infant newly born. It is something which, looked at objectively, is almost unbelievable; and yet, how often is this the attitude that we take up before God! We do not hesitate to assume, and to take it for granted, that we are capable of understanding everything that God does. We have such confidence in ourselves, and in our own minds and understandings and opinions, that we question and query God's actions in precisely the same way as we question the actions of fellow human beings. We feel, and we believe, that we know what is right and what is best. Our self-confidence is endless and boundless, and we refuse to believe that anything can possibly be beyond the reach and the grasp of our minds and intellects. This, surely, is the impertinent implication in all our questions, and in all our expressions of doubt. God is to conform to our ideas, and He is to do what we believe He should do. But the arrogance does not stop at that point. As we have seen, it does not hesitate to condemn God's actions and to say that they are quite wrong, and quite indefensible. In other words, we, and our ideas, are the standard and the judges. We are the ultimate court of appeal ; and our ideas of right and wrong, just and unjust, fair and unfair, are the last word. We do not hesitate to express our opinions about God, and to judge His actions. This is something of which the Children of Israel were constantly guilty. As we read of them in the Old Testament we are at times amazed and astonished at them. But how difficult to realise that we ourselves are guilty of precisely the same thing ! We may not express it with the same bluntness and rudeness, we may be more guarded and circumspect, and express it in the form of a question rather than in a direct statement. But all that is quite immaterial. In a matter like this, to harbour the thought for a moment is as reprehensible as to make the statement. It is not that I am saying that we must not think and reason in connection with religion, or that I am arguing that Christianity is irrational. We are meant to think and to reason and to grasp the truth. But that does not mean that our minds are equal to the mind of God, or that we can claim equality, and demand a full understanding of everything. Still less does it mean that, morally and spiritually, we are in a position to question and to query God's motives, and to pass judgment upon His character as expressed in His actions. And yet, that is precisely what men do. Failing to understand the actions, they proceed to attack and to question the very character of God. Our pride of intellect and of understanding leads us in reality to regard ourselves as gods. That is why I chose the term " arrogance " to describe this attitude. Oh ! the enormity of it all, the impertinence, the insolence ! There is but one explanation of it ; and that is, utter failure to realise Who and What God is, accompanied by utter failure to appreciate the truth about ourselves. If we only realised Whom we were questioning. If we but had some faint conception of the might, the greatness and the holiness of God ! And if we could realise our own utter nothingness, and insignificance, and helplessness. Try to consider it and to see it in the light of this passage. The relationship between God and ourselves is that of the Creator to the creature. He made us and gave us being. We had no part in the matter at all. We are the work of His hands, indeed we are to God what the clay is to the potter. Do you doubt it ? Well, let me ask you certain questions. What control have you really over your life ? You had no control over the beginning and you will have no control over the end. We have no idea as to how long we shall be here. Our lives are altogether in God's hands. We cannot control health and sickness, accidents and disease. We know not what a day may bring forth. Who could have foretold the present state of affairs ? Men have failed to prevent it. We are the creatures of time, and entirely subject to forces over which we have no control. We are quite helpless. As our Lord put it, we cannot " add one cubit to our stature." And yet we venture to try to measure God. How monstrous! Yea, how utterly mad! It means that our whole attitude is false and wrong. And it will remain such until we realise that God's " thoughts are not our thoughts " and that His " ways are not our ways," and until we accept His further statement that " as the heavens are higher than the earth, so are My ways higher than your ways, and My thoughts than your thoughts." Of necessity, there must be things therefore that we cannot understand and cannot fathom. Why, that is the whole glory of God's way of salvation ; and that is why it holds out a hope for all. You cannot understand ? You are tempted to question, and to argue, and to query ? The reply to you is, in the words of St. Paul, " Nay but, O man, who art thou that repliest against God ! shall the thing formed say to Him that formed it, why hast thou made me thus ? " " But that," you may say, " is not fair argument. It is rather a prohibition of argument, and the exertion of an unfair authority." To which I reply, that we were never meant to argue with God, and that we should never have started from the assumption that it was to be a discussion between two equal disputants. God is in heaven, and we are upon earth. God is holy, and we are sinful. God knows all things, and sees the end from the beginning.

We are ignorant and blind as the result of sin, and are the miserable slaves of time! Ultimately, that is the only theodicy that is necessary. A man who does not believe in God cannot possibly believe or understand the actions of God. But the more we believe truly in God, and realise increasingly His holy nature and character, the more shall we understand His ways. And even when we cannot understand, we shall be more and more ready to say with our blessed Lord " nevertheless not my will but Thine be done." There is a sense in which any attempt at a justification of God and His ways appears to me to be almost sinful, and I am tempted to say to any man who comes with his questions and criticisms, that his first business is not to try to understand God, but rather to understand himself and the life he is living. And having said that, I want to tell him that he had better consider the fleeting nature of his existence here on earth, and his entire dependence upon God Who is not only his Maker, but will also be his Judge. God needs no defence, for He is on The Throne. He is the Judge of all the earth. His Kingdom is without end. Cease to question and to argue! Bow down before Him! Worship Him! Get into the right attitude yourself, and you will begin to understand His actions. Oh, the arrogance of sin!

II. But such is the amazing love of God that He does not leave it at that. In spite of our sin and all its enormity, He deigns and condescends to reason with us, and to explain Himself to us. Nothing but Eternal Love could have such patience with such perverse and obstinate creatures. Here, we have a typical instance of such reasoning. It takes the form of *an exposure of the ignorance displayed in this attitude towards God.*

We have seen, already, that it is due to a fundamental failure to realise the nature of God, and of our true relationship to Him. But there are other ways in which our ignorance tends to lead us astray. We can illustrate them by shewing how this passage answers the various questions that have been raised, and gives knowledge which solves the various problems that tend to perplex the minds of men.

(*a*) The Children of Israel were questioning the power of God and wondering whether He could do anything to save them, and to save the situation, even as men tend in the same way, to-day, to query the power of God. What unutterable ignorance ! Listen ! " I have made the earth, and created man upon it : I, even my hands, have stretched out the heavens, and all their host have I commanded." That is the measure of His power. The God whom we worship, the God who is the Father of our Lord and Saviour Jesus Christ is also the Creator. By a mere word He made all things. He spoke and it happened. Read of His actions in the Old Testament, His mighty marvellous deeds. His very name " El " means the Strong or The Mighty One. Are you doubtful of His power to control men ? Isaiah has already given you the answer. " Behold the nations are as a drop of a bucket, and are counted as the small dust of the balance : behold, he taketh up the isles as a very little thing." " All nations before Him are as nothing : and they are counted to Him less than nothing, and vanity." And these are not mere words, not merely the result of a flight of poetic imagination. If you desire to be certain of their truth, read the secular history books which confirm the history and the teachings of the Old Testament. When Isaiah uttered those words the plight of Israel appeared to be hopeless. They were conquered, and were to be carried away to captivity by the greatest power the world had ever known. It seemed impossible that they should ever return. Nevertheless they did return. It was not their own action, they could do nothing ; it was simply a manifestation of the almighty power of God. But is not evil as a principle more powerful ? you may ask. The reply is : " I form the light and create darkness : I make peace and create evil, I, the Lord do all these things." " Creating evil " does not mean creating sin. It means that He made sorrow and misery and wretchedness to be the consequences and the results of sin. But even beyond that, the Bible teaches that sin and Satan are not beyond and outside the control of God. He permits them, but limits their activity, and, ultimately, He will destroy them. " Why does He allow them now ? " you ask. The answer, there, is " Nay but, O man, who art thou that repliest against God ? Shall the thing formed say to him

that formed it, Why hast thou made me thus ? "
We cannot tell, but this we know, that when death
and hell and evil exerted their maximum, their
full power against our Lord and Saviour Jesus
Christ, they were completely routed and defeated,
and by the mightiest manifestation of power the
world has ever known He rose triumphant from
the dead. " With God all things are possible."
He is the Almighty ; there is no limit to His power.

(b) But what of His love, His concern for us ?
The more we emphasise His power the more acutely
does this second question arise. Does He love us ?
Is He concerned about us? Why then does He
not do something ? Such were the questions asked
by Israel ; and men and women to-day ask the
same questions. God answers the questions by
revealing to the prophet what He was doing, and
what He proposed to do. He corrected the terrible
ignorance with respect to His love and His concern
for the people. He showed how He was working
quietly and unobtrusively all the time. " I have
raised him (Cyrus) up in righteousness, and I will
direct all his ways : he shall build my city, and he
shall let go my captives, not for price nor for
reward, saith the Lord of Hosts." They thought
He was doing nothing. The whole time He was
working and bringing His purposes to pass. Had
He forgotten Israel ? Was He not concerned
about them ? He had a great and a glorious
future in store for them, and to that end He was
making provision for them. In spite of their

disobedience and their sin, in spite of all that had been true of them and their attitude towards Him, God still loved Israel and was planning her salvation. Isaiah can no longer control himself. He cries out "Verily Thou art a God that hidest Thyself, O God of *Israel, the Saviour.*" He saw that God was still the God of Israel, and that as He had saved them from Egypt and the Red Sea, from the wilderness and their enemies, He would still save them from all calamities. And if you have believed on Him through Jesus Christ, if you have repented and accepted His great salvation, I assure you, that whatever may be happening to you, and however dark and difficult it may be, and however impossible to understand—I assure you that He is still your God, that He still loves you and cares for you, and that the promise still holds : " I will never leave thee nor forsake thee." Yea, as Peter put it so perfectly to those who were suffering tribulations and who could not quite understand, "Humble yourselves therefore under the mighty hand of God, that he may exalt you in due time : casting all your care upon him, for he careth for you." Never doubt that He careth.

(*c*) But perhaps our ignorance is greatest with respect to " the ways of God." This is a great theme in Isaiah as we have seen already in some of our quotations, and as we see so strikingly in our text. " His ways," are not " our ways." Because we cannot understand, we tend to doubt and to question. Oh! how foolish. "God moves

in a mysterious way His wonders to perform."
He appears to do the exact opposite of what we
should expect. He used a Cyrus, a Gentile, to
save the chosen people. At times He appears
to do nothing. Years and long periods pass and
God seems to be inactive, and in our impatience
we begin to cry out "How long?" God seems
to have lost control, and all seems to be going
wrong. Oh ! the folly of such thoughts. He
seemed to have forgotten the people in Egypt,
but He, in His own way and His own time, eventually
brought them out. He allowed them to be seventy
years in Babylon, but He had planned their return
to Jerusalem before they were ever taken captive.
For four hundred years the voice of the prophet
was still. Not a word after Malachi. But " when
the fulness of the time was come, God sent forth
His Son, made of a woman, made under the law,
to redeem them who were under the law, that we
might receive the adoption of sons." And so He
has continued to act throughout the ages. With
God " a thousand years are but as one day." In
His own time, and in His own way, He acts, He
works. Everything, all things, have been planned
" before the foundation of the world." The scheme
is perfect, the plan is complete. Nothing will
fail. Read the story of the past and see how it
confirms the prophecies. Then read the prophecies
with respect to the future. Having done so, you
will laugh at your fears and alarms, your evil forebodings and your questionings, and you will cry

out with Isaiah, "Verily Thou art a God that hidest Thyself, O God of Israel, the Saviour."

What else can you say ? What else can be said ? Is there any other comment that is adequate to the situation ? There is but one, and it is even greater, that mighty word of St. Paul as he contemplated God's future plan for Israel and the world : " O the depth of the riches both of the wisdom and the knowledge of God ! How unsearchable are his judgments, and his ways past finding out ! For who hath known the mind of the Lord ? or who hath been His counsellor ? Or who hath first given to him, and it shall be recompensed unto him again ? For of him, and through him, and to him, are all things : to whom be glory for ever, Amen." And let us add, Amen and Amen !

IV

WHY DOES GOD ALLOW WAR?

WHY DOES GOD ALLOW WAR?

JAMES iv. 1

" From whence come wars and fightings among you ? come they not hence, even of your lusts that war in your members ? "

IT is interesting and strange to note that in what may be termed the religious attitude towards the war, or the attitude of religious people towards the war, two tendencies almost invariably manifest themselves. The first is the tendency to discuss the whole question of war almost entirely apart from God, or at any rate in a manner in which the problem of war is only related to God in a very indirect manner. Regarding war only and solely from the human angle, those who take up this attitude are very concerned about, and preoccupied with, the various problems of human conduct that are raised by war. They are much interested in the question as to what the Christian's attitude should be, that is, as to how war should affect man. They try to discover the causes of war in general, and any particular war that may take place. They immerse themselves in political, economic, psychological and philosophical theories which claim that they hold the key to the mystery.

And they try to apply this knowledge to any concrete instance. Having done so, and believing passionately that it is the business of religion to produce a just and a lasting peace, they proceed to discuss the various measures that should be adopted in order to bring that to pass. In this group are to be found those who style themselves pacifists as well as many who are definitely not pacifists. The interest is primarily and almost entirely in war as it affects man, and especially the man who claims the name of Christian. Should he take part or not? What kind of peace terms should he advocate? etc., etc. Such are the issues which are uppermost in their minds; and even though they may stress and emphasise the spiritual or the Christian aspect, as they see it, to the maximum, still it is true to say of them that the question of the direct relationship of God to war is practically never considered by them at all. That they may reply to the effect that of course they have taken that as a fundamental postulate, and have assumed that the very idea of war is abhorrent to God, and of necessity has nothing to do directly with God because it is the result of man's sin and folly—that they say all this, far from disposing of what we have said, rather tends to confirm it. God's attitude to war is taken for granted and is therefore not discussed; war is regarded as a problem which is altogether and entirely on the human plane and level—a merely human question and problem.

The second tendency is the exact opposite. Here,

the one great interest is the question of the direct relationship of God to war. In a subsidiary way, those who belong to this group may also be interested in some of the questions to which we have referred. But their one big problem, their real difficulty, is not " How does war affect man ? " but rather, " How is war to be fitted in to God's governance of this world ? " In a word, what perplexes these people most of all is not the explanation of the origin of war or their own immediate duty with respect to it : what they desire to know is " Why does God allow or permit war ? " That to them is the question of all questions, because on the answer to it depends the whole of their belief in God. And obviously, if that is in doubt, all other questions become somewhat irrelevant and unnecessary.

We are concerned in this study with this second attitude. We have been considering together in the previous chapters various problems with regard to the general difficulty of understanding God's ways. In all those instances we have been con-cerned most especially with the subjective problem of God's dealing with us directly. But here, at this point, we come to a more objective problem. It may be that at the back of it lies the subjective question of why God allows war in view of what it means to us ; but the question in the forefront is certainly the strictly objective one of reconciling our belief in God with the fact that God allows war. That I suppose, was the question that was asked most frequently during the 1914-18 war. I have the impression, whether rightly or wrongly I do not know, that it is not being asked quite so frequently during this present war. If so, I fear it is due to the fact that godlessness has been greatly on the increase, and also to the fact that, in our preoccupation with ourselves and our own actions, much of our religion has become godless and has degenerated into a mere matter of attitudes, opinions, ideas and actions. However, there are many who are asking the question to-day, and it is therefore our duty to deal with it.

The people who ask this question can, I believe, be classified into three main groups. First of all we have the type who ask it rather defiantly and arrogantly, as if to suggest that this is the final proof, either of the fact that there is no God at all, or else that if there is a God, He is clearly not a God of love. Their question is a statement rather than a query. As we have already indicated on previous occasions, the real difficulty here is the fundamental one of belief in God at all. The whole attitude is wrong ; and what is needed on our part and from our side is not so much a theodicy with respect to the particular question of war, as a statement which is likely to lead to repentance, and an acceptance of God's salvation by faith in Jesus Christ. There is no purpose whatever in arguing about a particular and subsidiary question with a person who is clearly not right on the central question. If a man does not believe in God it is idle to discuss with him one of God's actions.

We only try to explain the ways of God to those who believe in Him and who are in a genuine and honest perplexity.

That brings us to the second type of person who asks this question. Here we have what may be called the pietistic type of Christian. This person is far removed from the one we have just been considering. It cannot be said of him that his belief in God is so slight and so slender that the merest suspicion of an ill wind can destroy and sever it. He has been orthodox, and has believed all that Christians should believe. More, he has enjoyed his religion and has found in it the main interest of his life. But the interest has been almost entirely personal—personal in the sense of an experience of personal salvation, personal also in the sense that the directly experimental and experiential results and effects of Christianity have been the main objects of consideration and of interest. This has been true even with respect to his study of the Bible. He has gone to it for food for his soul in a personal sense, and the type of commentary that has appealed to him most of all has been that which is classified as " devotional." Theology has not interested him. Indeed, he may have felt it to be a danger. Christianity as a " world view " is literally something that has never entered into his ken at all. His tendency has been to shut himself off from the world, intellectually as well as in practice. And still more important, he has tended to dissociate God from any interest in the world save in the redeemed. And as long as there was peace all was well. But the outbreak of war forces upon this type of person the consideration of the larger problem ; and for the first time he may have to ask himself whether his scheme of things can include this. Not having faced it before, such a person often finds himself in real difficulties, and especially when he discusses the question with the other type of person whom we have already considered. God in personal salvation in Christ he can understand—but God allowing war ?

The third type that is perplexed by this matter, is the kind of person who has held certain vague and loose ideas about God and about the nature of God. They have singled out the love of God from all His other attributes, and they have stressed it at the expense of the others, and often to the entire exclusion of the others. Their ideas about the love of God, moreover, are sentimental and weak. This shows itself in normal times in the view they hold of the subject of forgiveness, their representation being that God as love forgives without any conditions whatsoever, as if His righteousness and holiness were non-existent. The idea that God should under any circumstances punish is altogether foreign to their whole outlook. The one activity they recognise in God is His forgiveness, and His benevolent attitude towards mankind. Holding this view of God, and believing thus, that God's one idea is that men and women shall be happy at all costs, they cannot understand how God can possibly allow war with all its cruelty and its suffering. It seems to them to be incompatible with all that they have previously believed.

Now these last two positions deserve our sympathetic consideration. They are genuine and honest difficulties which actually give rise to pain as well as to intellectual perplexity. What have we to say to them? Obviously, in the space of one sermon we cannot hope to deal with the matter in any exhaustive manner. We can simply lay down the general principles which are taught so clearly in the Bible, comparing scripture with scripture. Incidentally, it is interesting to observe that this actual question of " Why does God allow war ? " is not considered or raised as such in the Bible at all. The text we have chosen is the nearest approach to it ; for it does raise the question of the origin of war, though it deals with the matter from the standpoint of ourselves rather than from the other angle, with which we are mainly concerned. Our business in this study, then, will be, not so much to expound this particular text, as to deal with the general teaching of the Bible on the subject. The most convenient division of the matter is to divide our answer into the negative and the positive.

A. *By the negative answer* we mean not that God does not allow war, as if to suggest that He is not able to do so, or that it is something which is altogether outside His control. We mean, that before we come to deal with the teaching of the Bible on the matter positively, it is important that we should examine the complaint that is made, and show how it is based upon certain false pre-suppositions. We shall deal with but two of these.

(1) There can be no doubt at all that most of the trouble arises from the fact that so many, instead of taking the teaching of the Bible as it is, and, indeed, oftentimes not even taking the trouble to read the Bible at all, in order to discover its teaching, absorb certain ideas that are loudly proclaimed and freely taught. As we have already indicated, that is probably the reason why the question has been raised more frequently and more seriously in this century than in previous times. Formerly, theology and the practical living of the Christian life were based directly on the Bible and its teaching. But latterly the approach has been more and more philosophical, and men, having drawn a false picture of God, are surprised and annoyed that facts seem to demonstrate that the drawing is not accurate ! Men who read and who knew their Bible, and who lived by its teaching, were not worried and perplexed by the problem of war in its relation to God. They did not feel that it assailed the very roots and foundations of their faith. Why ? Because they saw clearly that the Bible nowhere and never promises that there shall be no war, at any rate this side of the millennium. Indeed, they observed further that its teaching seemed to be the exact opposite. They saw how our Lord Himself prophesied that right until the

end of the age, and especially as the final consummation drew nearer and nearer there would be " wars and rumours of wars." His words actually were (Matthew xxiv. 6, 7) : " And ye shall hear of wars and rumours of wars ; see that ye be not troubled : for all these things must come to pass, but the end is not yet. For nation shall rise against nation, and kingdom against kingdom : and there shall be famines and pestilences and earthquakes in divers places." They remembered also the dark and mysterious prophecies of the Book of Revelation, all pointing in the same direction. They thought also of those words of St. Paul, where he said that evil men should wax " worse and worse " and that " the mystery of iniquity " which was already working would later be let loose and work without restraint. The idea that the world, partly as the result of its own inner momentum, and partly as the result of the preaching of the gospel and in accordance with the general plan and desire of God, would gradually evolve into a better and better place, is entirely false to the teaching of the Bible itself. Yet that has been the popular teaching for many years, teaching which has impregnated not only the minds of the majority outside the Church, but, one feels at times, the majority of those within the Church also. We have been told over and over again that, as men grasped the purpose of God as offered and taught to them by the various educational and cultural agencies, the time would soon be at hand when wars would be no more and we should all live in a state of peace and plenty and universal happiness. Indeed, it has been argued that if man with his intelligence and enlightenment can come to see the folly and the horror of war, and do his all to prevent war, then God of necessity must hate it to an infinitely greater degree, and must obviously, therefore, restrain and prevent it. If we were making all this effort to produce a perfect world, free from war, God surely must be doing so to a still greater extent.

So the argument ran ; and its acceptance has been very widespread. Some believed it actively ; others, quite unconsciously and without really thinking about it at all, and without any testing, allowed themselves to believe it. The dogma was that God must be working with all His might to prevent war. It was part and parcel of the view held of God. The reply is, as we have seen, that it is a purely imaginary idea. God has not promised us such a world. He has actually taught us to expect the very kind of world in which we are living to-day. The words of our Lord were " see that ye be not troubled." Being forewarned, we were to be fore-armed in the realm of our minds and spirits. If we take the Bible and its records as the supreme revelation of God, the fact of war should not trouble us in the sense that it will shake our faith in God. The Biblical " world view " is thoroughly pessimistic. Nothing is so important as that we should study the Bible itself and discover what God proposes to do for this world, and what God has promised to do for this world, instead of projecting our own hopes and desires and wishes into and on to God's plans, and then be surprised and disappointed and grieved when we discover that they are not being carried out. So our first reply to the question " Why does God allow war ? " is to ask another question— " Has God ever promised to prevent or to prohibit war ? "

(2) Our second answer may also be put in the form of a question : " Why do we expect God to prohibit war ? " or " Why *should* God prevent war ? " Apart from the theoretical reason that God should prevent war because it is sinful, with which we shall deal in the next section, there can be no doubt that the real reason why people expect God to prevent war, is that they desire a state of peace, and feel that they have the right to live in a state of peace. But that immediately raises another question, which, in a sense, is the fundamental question with respect to this whole matter. " What right have we to peace ? " " Why do we desire peace ? " How often, I wonder, have we faced this question ? Has not the tendency been to take it for granted that we have a right to a state and condition of peace ? Do we stop to ask what is the real value and purpose and function of peace ? This question, surely, should have engaged our attention, and especially during the past twelve months, when, having escaped the outbreak of war by a very narrow margin, we were constantly face to face with the possibility of the

outbreak of war. There are two passages, at least, in scripture which show very clearly why we should desire peace. The first is in Acts ix. 31 : " Then had the churches rest throughout all Judea and Galilee and Samaria, and were edified ; and walking in the fear of the Lord, and in the comfort of the Holy Ghost, were multiplied." That is a description of what happened in the churches after a terrible period of persecution and unrest. We should desire peace in order that what is described there may happen amongst us also. The other passage is in 1 Timothy ii. 1, 2 : " I exhort therefore, that, first of all, supplications, prayers, intercessions and giving of thanks, be made for all men, for kings, and for all that are in authority, that we may lead a quiet and a peaceable life in all godliness and honesty." There we have the same emphasis again. It is not enough that we should desire peace merely that we may avoid the horror and the suffering of war, and all the dislocations and hardships and interference with ordinary life that are consequent upon it. Our real desire for peace should be based upon the further desire to have the fullest opportunity to live the godly and the holy life, and to have the maximum amount of time in which to build ourselves up in the faith. Man's chief business in life is to serve and to glorify God. That is why the gift of life has been given to him. That is why we are here on earth ; all other things are subservient to this—all the gifts and the pleasures which God gives us so freely. That is the chief end and object of man's life; and consequently he should desire peace because it enables him to do that more freely and fully than he can during a state of war. But is that our reason for desiring peace? Has that been the reason during the past year? Has that been the real motive in our prayers for peace? It is not for me to judge, but one cannot be blind to facts. Far too often, I fear, the motive has been purely selfish—merely the avoidance of the consequences of war. Indeed, it has frequently failed to rise even to that level, and one has felt that many have desired peace merely in order to avoid a disturbance of the kind of life which they were living and enjoying so heartily. What kind of life was that? In a word, it was almost the exact opposite of that described in our two passages of scripture. Under the blessing of peace since the 1914-18 war, men and women, in constantly increasing numbers, have forsaken God and religion and have settled down to a life which is essentially materialistic and sinful. Thinking that the 1914-18 war was indeed "the war to end war," with a false sense of security, buttressed also by insurance schemes and various other provisions to safeguard themselves against the possible dangers that still remained, men and women in this and in every other country gave themselves to a life of pleasure-seeking, accompanied by spiritual and mental indolence. This became evident not only in the decline in religion, but still more markedly in the appalling decline in morals; and indeed, finally, even in a decline in a political and social sense. It was a life of purely selfish and carnal enjoyment, with all the slackness in every respect that such a life always produces. It led to the decadence on which the rulers of Germany banked, and on which they based their calculations. They did not believe that we would not fight because we were highly spiritual, but, rather, because they felt that we had lost our stamina and would allow nothing to interfere with our indolent life. Then came a crisis in September, 1938. Men and women crowded to places of worship and prayed for peace. Afterwards they assembled to thank God for peace. But was it because they had decided to use peace for the one and only true purpose, namely, to " live a quiet and peaceable life in all godliness and honesty " ? Was it in order that they might walk " in the fear of the Lord and in the comfort of the Holy Ghost " ? The facts speak for themselves. Thus I ask the questions : Had we a right to peace ? Do we deserve peace ? Were we justified in asking God to preserve peace and to grant peace ? What if war has come because we were not fit for peace, because we did not deserve peace ; because we by our disobedience and godlessness and sinfulness had so utterly abused the blessings of peace ? Have we a right to expect God to preserve a state of peace merely to allow men and women to continue a life that is an insult to His Holy Name ?

B. But that leads us to a consideration of what we have called *the positive answer* to this great question. That God allows war is a fact. Why does He allow it ? What is the positive treatment of this question in the Bible ? Here it is not so much a question of specific statements, as of applying certain fundamental principles, clearly taught, to this particular issue.

(1) We must consider, first, what we may call the *Biblical view of war*. It is not that war as such is sin, but that war is a consequence of sin ; or, if you prefer it, that war is one of the expressions of sin. Actually from the point of view of a theodicy that distinction really does not matter, as the argument still remains the same. The Bible traces war back to its final and ultimate cause. It is true that it does not altogether ignore the various political and social and economic and psychological factors of which so much has been made. But according to its teaching, these things are no more than the immediate causes, the actual agencies employed. The thing itself is much deeper. As James reminds us, the ultimate cause of war is lust and desire ; this restlessness that is a part of us as the result of sin ; this craving for that which is illicit and for that which we cannot obtain. It shows itself in many ways, both in personal, individual life, and also in the life of nations. It is the root cause of theft and robbery, jealousy and envy, pride and hate, infidelity and divorce. And in precisely the same way it leads to personal quarrels and strife, and also to wars between nations. The Bible does not isolate war, as if it were something separate and

unique and quite apart, as we tend to do in our thinking. It is but one of the manifestations of sin, one of the consequences of sin. On a larger scale, perhaps, and in a more terrible form for that reason, but still, in its essence, precisely the same as all the other effects and consequences of sin. But someone may argue that there must be an essential difference because of the fact that loss of life is involved in war. The reply is, that while the Bible regards life as sacred, and prohibits us to take life merely to gratify a spirit of lust or of revenge, it at the same time teaches that, from God's side, the soul is of infinitely greater importance than the life of the body. God's concern is not that our lives should be perpetuated and prolonged here on earth for a certain number of additional years, but rather that we should come into the right relationship with Him, and live lives that will glorify His Holy Name. We attach such significance to time, and to length of years, that we tend to forget that what ultimately matters and counts is the quality of the life. War, then, is a consequence and an effect of sin of precisely the same kind as all the other effects and consequences of sin. Sin always leads to suffering, misery and shame, whether in a quiet or in a spectacular manner. We tend to become concerned when the principle manifests itself in bulk or on a large scale. We ignore it or fail to see it in its real essence, which is what really matters. To ask God to prohibit war or to prevent war, therefore, is to ask Him to

96

prohibit one of the particular consequences of sin. Or, if we take the view that war itself is actual sin, it is to ask God to prohibit one particular sin. Here again we see both the selfishness that is involved in the request and also the insult to God. Because this particular form of sin, or consequence of sin, is especially painful and difficult for us, we ask God to prohibit it. We are not at all concerned about the holiness of God, or sin as such. Were we so concerned, we would ask Him to prohibit all sin and to restrain all iniquity. We would ask Him to prohibit drunkenness, gambling, immorality and vice, the breaking of the Sabbath, and all the various other sins which men enjoy so thoroughly. But if anyone ventured to suggest that, a protest loud and strong would be registered immediately in the name of freedom. We boast of our free-will and resent any suggestion or teaching that God should in any way interfere with it. And yet, when, as the result of the exercise of that very freedom, we find ourselves faced with the horrors and troubles and sufferings of a war, like peevish children we cry out our protests and complain bitterly against God because He has not used His almighty power and forcibly prevented it ! God, in His infinite and everlasting wisdom, has decided not to prohibit sin and not to restrain altogether the consequences of sin. War is not an isolated and separate spiritual and religious problem. It is just a part and an expression of the one great central problem of sin.

(2) But the Biblical teaching advances beyond

that point, and gives reasons which are still more positive in explanation of the fact that God allows war. We shall merely tabulate them.

(a) It is clear that God permits war in order that men may bear the consequences of their sins as punishment. This is a fundamental law which expresses itself in such words as " whatsoever a man soweth that shall he also reap." Punishment is not altogether postponed to the next world. Here, in this world, we bear some of the punishment for our sins. How clearly is this shown time and time again in the story of the Children of Israel ! They disobeyed God and flouted His holy laws. For a while all was well. But then they began to suffer. God withdrew His protecting care from them, and they were at the mercy of their enemies, who attacked them and robbed them. Indeed, at the very beginning, and as the result of the first sin and transgression, we find that God ordained and decreed punishment. God said, " Cursed is the ground for thy sake ; in sorrow shalt thou eat of it all the days of thy life." Every painful consequence of sin is a part of the punishment meted out for sin. But someone may raise the objection, and ask : " But why do the innocent suffer ? " The answer cannot be given fully here, but in its essence it is twofold. First, there is no such person as the innocent, as we have seen already. We are all sinful. But furthermore, we clearly have to reap the consequences not only of our own personal sins, but also of the sins of the entire race; and, on a smaller scale, the sins of our particular country or group. We are, at one and the same time, individuals, and members of the state and of the entire race. The Gospel saves us as individuals ; but that does not mean that we cease to be members of the state and part and parcel of the entire human race. We share the same sun and rain as other people, and we are exposed to the same illnesses and diseases. We are subject to the same trials by way of industrial depression and other causes of unhappiness, including war. Thus it comes to pass that the innocent may have to bear part of the punishment for sins for which they are not directly responsible.

(b) Again, it seems clear that God permits war in order that men may see through it, more clearly than they have ever done before, what sin really is. In times of peace we tend to think lightly of sin, and to hold optimistic views of human nature. War reveals man and the possibilities within man's nature. The 1914-18 war shattered that optimistic view of man which had held sway for so many years, and revealed something of the essential sinfulness of human nature. One of the direct consequences of that has been the theological revival on the continent of Europe, associated with the name of Karl Barth. A time of crisis and of war is no time for superficial generalisations and for rosy, optimistic idealisms. It forces us to examine the very foundations of life. It makes us face the direct question as to what it is in human nature that leads to such calamities. The explanation cannot be found in the actions of certain men only. It is something deep down in the heart of man, in the heart of all men. It is the selfishness, hatred, jealousy, envy, bitterness and malice that are in the human heart and which show themselves in the personal and social relationships of life, manifesting themselves on a national and international scale. In the personal sphere we tend to excuse them and to explain them away. But on the larger scale they become more evident. Man in his pride and his folly refuses to listen to the positive teaching of the Gospel about sin. He refuses to attend a place of worship, and refuses instruction from the Word of God. He rejects the gracious, loving offer of the Gospel. He believes that he knows himself, and thinks that he is capable of making a perfect world altogether without God. What he refuses to recognise and to learn by the preaching of the Gospel in a time of peace, God reveals to him by permitting war ; and thereby shows him his true nature and the result of his sin. What man refuses and rejects when offered by the hand of love, he often takes when delivered to him through the medium of affliction.

(c) And all this, in turn, leads to the final purpose, which is to lead us back to God. Like the Prodigal Son, when we have lost all and are suffering acutely and in a state of wretchedness and misery, seeing our folly and our stupidity, we think of God, even as he thought of his father and his home. No word is found more frequently in the Old Testament as a description of the Children of Israel than the words, " in their trouble and distresses they cried unto the Lord." They were blind to the goodness and the kindness of God ; they turned a deaf ear to the appeals of His love and His grace ; but in their agony they remembered Him, and turned to Him. And we are still the same. It is only as we suffer and see our folly, and the utter bankruptcy and helplessness of men, that we shall turn to God and rely upon Him. Indeed, as I contemplate human nature and human life, what astonishes me is not that God allows and permits war, but the patience and the long-suffering of God. " He maketh his sun to rise on the evil and on the good, and sendeth rain on the just and the unjust." He suffered the evil, perverse ways of the Children of Israel for centuries ; and now for nearly two thousand years He has patiently borne with a world which in the main rejects and refuses His loving offer, even in the Person of His only-begotten Son. The question that needs to be asked is not " Why does God allow war ? " but rather, " Why does God not allow the world to destroy itself entirely in its iniquity and its sin ? Why does He in His restraining grace set a limit to evil and to sin, and a bound beyond which they cannot pass ? " Oh, the amazing patience of God with this sinful world ! How wondrous is His love ! He has sent the Son of His love to our world to die for us and to save us ; and because men cannot and will not see this, He permits and allows such things as war to chastise and to punish us ; to teach us, and to convict us of our sins ; and, above all, to call us to repentance and acceptance of His gracious offer. The vital question for us therefore is not to ask, " Why does God allow war ? " The question for us is to make sure that we are learning the lesson, and repenting before God for the sin in our own hearts, and in the entire human race, which leads to such results. May God grant us understanding and the true spirit of repentance, for His Name's sake.

V

THE FINAL ANSWER TO ALL OUR QUESTIONS

THE FINAL ANSWER TO ALL OUR QUESTIONS

ROMANS viii. 28

" And we know that all things work together for good to them that love God, to them who are the called according to his purpose."

HERE, perhaps, in the briefest compass, we have the most comprehensive, and the most final, answer to all the various questionings and complaints that tend to rise within our minds and our hearts during a time of trial and of difficulty. The apostle was writing to men and women who were suffering hardships, and experiencing trials and tribulations. These things were trying and testing their faith. They wondered why they were being allowed to endure them, and they were still more baffled as to how these things could be reconciled with the promises which had been held before them in the Gospel. St. Paul deals with the whole question in this mighty passage. He has, in the earlier part of the chapter, been working out the results and the fruits of the Gospel in the personal life of the believer. He has shown how, as the result of the working of the Holy Spirit, the believer is enabled to become more than

105

conqueror over all the assaults of flesh and sin. Then he proceeds to show how the Holy Spirit, in addition to that, also gives us the assurance of sonship, testifying with our spirit that we are the children of God, and therefore heirs and joint-heirs with Christ. Then, suddenly, at verse 18 he introduces the statement, " For I reckon that the sufferings of this present time are not worthy to be compared with the glory which shall be revealed in us." Why does he say that ? The answer must be that he imagines someone in Rome arguing in the following manner : " It is all very well for you to hold before us that glorious vision and to tell us that we are heirs of God and joint-heirs with Christ. But look at our situation, see the things that are happening to us and the things that are threatening us in the future ! Do they indicate that God is taking a special interest in us ? Do they augur a future bright with promises ? Everything seems to be against us. Far from occupying the customary position of heirs, we are confronted daily by tribulation, distress, persecution, famine, nakedness, peril and the sword. How are these things to be reconciled with the great and precious promises of which you write and of which you speak ? Have we any guarantee that, in spite of all that is happening to us, what you say will ultimately come to pass ? " That being the difficulty, either actual or conceivable, in the minds of the Christians at Rome, St. Paul proceeds to deal with it and to give the answer to it. This is surely one of the most magnificent passages that is to be found in his writings. As a piece of literature it is superb. As apologetic, as an eloquent and, at the same time, reasoned and logical statement of a case it is masterly. And, above all, there breathes through it a spirit of devout worship. It is not an academic or theoretical discourse on a problem. The writer himself has experienced untold difficulties and trials. He has been in prison frequently, has been beaten with stripes above measure, has several times been face to face with death, has of the Jews five times received forty stripes save one, has been beaten with rods and stoned, has three times suffered shipwreck and been in the deep " a night and a day," has been " in perils of waters, in perils of robbers, in perils by mine own countrymen, in perils by the heathen, in perils in the city, in perils in the wilderness, in perils in the sea, in perils among false brethren, in weariness and painfulness, in watchings often, in hunger and thirst, in fastings often, in cold and nakedness." That has been his experience ; and he writes to men and women who, while they had not suffered in the way that he had, nevertheless were having a very difficult time.

There is a sense in which we should consider the entire passage as a whole. But the text before us focuses attention on the central principles, which are taught not only here, but also everywhere else in the New Testament. This passage is typical of the New Testament method of comforting and consoling believers. It is vitally important that we should observe carefully and precisely what it does say, and also what it does not say. We must be careful not to allow the writer's eloquence to carry us away, and not to be content merely with some general feeling. We must analyse the statement and see exactly what it has to say. But before we do that, there is something else which we must do and which, in a sense, is quite as important. We must observe not only the actual statement, but also the way in which the statement is made. Or, if you prefer it, the method of the theodicy is as important as the details of the theodicy. Or, to use still another form of expression, we must grasp the principles on which the statement is founded as well as the details of the statement. Indeed, if we fail to do this, whatever effect these words may produce upon us will be false, and entirely foreign to what was in the Apostle's mind.

There are two main principles which are absolutely vital to a true understanding and grasping of the New Testament teaching with respect to this whole matter of consolation and comfort. The first is that the comfort it imparts is always *theological*. That statement may well arouse feelings of surprise, and indeed of annoyance, in many. For it cuts right across what we should naturally expect, and it is certainly the extreme opposite of what has been the popular attitude towards religion for some time. We have referred already, several times, during our consideration of this general theme of theodicy, to the opposition to theology and to systematic teaching and thinking. Experience and results have been unduly exalted, and any attempt to stress the vital importance of a true foundation has been resented, and has been dismissed as indicative of a rational or legalistic outlook. But apart from the general opposition to theology, there are many who, I say, are surprised and pained at the thought that theology should have a vital place in this matter of comfort and of consolation. Their position is, that they can well see the importance of having a basis to one's life, and that there is undoubtedly a need for theology and definition. " Such," they argue, " may well occupy our time and attention during a time of peace and of tranquillity. But during a time of trial and affliction, a time of crises and of stress," they proceed, "what one needs is not a theological thesis or reasoned statement, but comfort and consolation. When nerves are frayed and minds are tired, when feelings are wounded and hearts are at the breaking point, it is surely cruel to present men and women with some sort of a compendium of theology. They need to be made to feel happier and brighter ; they need help to forget their problems and their troubles. They need to be soothed and eased. Theological terms at such a time are an impertinence, however right they may be during normal times." This is a very widespread feeling. How terribly and tragically wrong it is, how utterly false to the New Testament, is shown plainly in this great passage. It is surely one of the most highly theological passages in the Bible.

Listen to some of the terms that are used. " Fore-knowledge," " predestination," " justification," " glorification," " the elect " ! These are the great and characteristic words of theology, the words that have been hated and abominated so heartily by all who demand and insist upon a " religion that does something." Yet these are the words which are used as an integral part of his message by this loving apostle, who had himself suffered so much, as he writes to men and women who were exposed to sufferings and trials which we can scarcely imagine. He conveys his comfort and consolation to them in this passage which probably contains more pure theology, and which has probably led to more argument and discussion and disputation, than any other individual passage in the whole of the Bible. Why does he do that ? And what does it mean ? The answer is twofold.

It means that the New Testament never isolates the problem of happiness, and never deals with it as if it were something separate and special which could be handled on its own. We, desiring happiness as we do, tend to do the opposite. We approach happiness directly and immediately. We fail to realise that happiness according to the New Testament is always the result of something else, and that what determines, therefore, whether it is true or false is the nature of the agent which produces it. According to the New Testament there is but one real happiness or joy, and that is the happiness that is based upon a true relationship to

110

God, the happiness which is the result of the righteousness that God gives us through Jesus Christ His Son. It is because we have false notions of happiness, and base it upon false and insecure foundations, that we so constantly experience alternating periods of elation and dejection, joy and despair. The only joy that never fails is that which is given by the Lord Himself according to His promise. The way to obtain it, and to retain it, therefore, is to understand and to grasp the conditions on which He gives it. And that implies thought and theology.

The other reason why St. Paul offers his consolation in this way, is that he was anxious that they should grasp the method whereby he consoled and comforted himself, in order that they might apply it to themselves whenever, and wherever, occasion might arise in the future. He was not out to comfort them, and to make them feel happy merely while they were reading the letter, or while they were still under the influence of his personality. For that would have meant that he would have to write to them regularly at intervals. But he might not be alive to do so, and they might be scattered and cast into prison, and be beyond the reach of letters. He desires, therefore, to introduce them to the method which can be applied always, and everywhere, and in spite of all circumstances and conditions. The happiness of the Christian, he would have them see, is not to be something which is produced artificially and which is dependent upon circumstances and surroundings which may be constantly changing. It is to be the result of an acceptance of certain truths, and the working out of a reasoned, logical argument on the basis of these truths. It is not to be something vague, and general, and intangible, which varies with one's moods and feelings, or with the precise situation in which one finds oneself. It is not to be dependent even upon regular attendance at the House of God, and the effect of its atmosphere, or the preaching of its preachers. It is to be the result of an argument, the end and conclusion of a logical series of positions which any believer can, and must, work out for himself. If we depend upon anything save an understanding of the truth, we are doomed ultimately to disappointment and unhappiness. But, if we accept the truth and grasp its teaching, we shall be able to apply it to our needs at all times and in all places. The primary business of the Church with respect to believers is to teach the doctrines of the faith, and not merely to try to enthuse or to comfort in general.

The second principle which is always in evidence in the comforting and consolatory passages of the New Testament is the view which it takes of life. That view is what is generally termed " other-worldly " or spiritual. Failure to realise that this is so, surely accounts for much of the unhappiness in the lives of Christian people, and also for much of the sense of disappointment that they feel when certain unpleasant experiences fall to their lot. And yet there is nothing which is quite so characteristic of the Bible as this view which it takes of life. This is seen very clearly in this passage with which we are dealing. Christians, according to St. Paul, are " heirs." They have not yet inherited fully, they are waiting, they are expecting. There is " a glory which is to be revealed," and they look forward to it. They are " waiting for the adoption, to wit, the redemption of the body." They have not yet gathered in the great harvest, but they have received " the first-fruits." They have not yet seen fully their great inheritance, but they have seen and known sufficient to make them hope for the remainder, and, hoping for that, they " in patience do wait for it." And it is because of all this, that St. Paul can say with such confidence that, he " reckons that the sufferings of this present time are not worthy to be compared with the glory which shall be revealed in us." Though he lives *in* the present it is clear that the Christian, according to St. Paul, is meant to live *for* the future. That is why he tells him elsewhere to " set his affection on things above, not on things on the earth," and exhorts the Ephesians to know " what is the hope of his calling and the riches of the glory of his inheritance in the saints." This is also the view that we find in the Epistle to the Hebrews, especially in chapters XI and XII. And in like manner we remember how St. Peter talks about " the living and the lively hope." Indeed, it is the view of life found everywhere in the New Testament and also in the Old Testament. The true believers in Israel regarded themselves as " pilgrims and strangers," on the earth, mere sojourners in this land of time. They were all looking forward and looking ahead ; they were pilgrims on their way to God and to eternity. That is the view of life held everywhere in the Bible, and that view is vital to its comforting and consolatory teaching. Indeed, without this, there is no comfort at all. The New Testament is primarily interested in the condition of our souls, not our bodies ; its concern is with our spiritual welfare rather than with our material condition ; and, over and above, and before it begins to consider our relationship to men and what they may do to us, it stresses the all-importance of a right relationship to God. The result is, that it seems to ride very loosely to this present life and to this present world ; and, face to face with the worst conditions conceivable, it can boldly say "The Lord is my helper, and I will not fear what man shall do unto me," and " For our light affliction, which is but for a moment, worketh for us a far more exceeding and eternal weight of glory. While we look not at the things which are seen but at the things which are not seen, for the things which are seen are temporal but the things which are not seen are eternal." That is its attitude towards life. We need not indicate how totally different this is from the modern view which is almost altogether " this-worldly." Looking and hoping for things in this life and in this world, men and women are disappointed, and, in turn, tend to blame God and the gospel. And when they are reminded that it is their life and world views which are false and not true to the Biblical teaching, they reply by stating that the other-worldly view is nothing but a manifestation of escapism, and at the same time is guilty of neglecting present conditions and problems. The answer to that charge cannot be given fully in a passing word, but we must show that it is an entirely false charge. This we can do by first reminding you of certain historical facts. Can the people whose lives we find recorded in the Old Testament be described as men and women who avoided the problems of life—your Abraham, Jacob, Moses, David and all the others ? Can it be said of the apostles, and especially of St. Paul, that holding this other-worldly view they just escaped from, and avoided, the problems and the responsibilities of life in this world ? And afterwards, can that charge be levelled at the Puritans who perhaps, above all others, exemplified this view of life ?

That Christians who hold the other-worldly view refuse to become excited about, and to work for, ideas and schemes which are based upon the precise opposite view of life, does not mean that they are unconcerned about life and what happens in it. Their position is, that they have learned that the greatest of all snares is to be bound by this world, and to live only for this life. They have had a vision of things " which eye hath not seen

115

nor ear heard and which have not entered into the heart of man." They live for these things and their ultimate attainment. These are the things that enthuse them. Indeed, these are the things by which they live. But that does not mean entire indifference to this world. It means and implies a very pessimistic view of this world, accompanied by efforts to make it as tolerable as is possible.

Are we as concerned about our souls as we are about our bodies? Do we experience as much agony of spirit as we contemplate the terrible spiritual warfare that is going on in this world at all times, as we do with respect to the physical wars that take place from time to time? Can we say that we grieve as much about the wrong relationship of men to God as we do about broken national and international relationships? If our view of life is not that of the New Testament, we shall not only experience grievous disappointments in this world, but we shall also fail to be comforted and consoled by its teaching.

Having considered in that way the vitally important background to our text, we can proceed to look at its specific and detailed teaching along the following lines. In the face of all kinds of trials, and tribulations, and difficulties, it announces that " all things work together for good to them that love God, to them who are the called according to his purpose." This is both a statement and a promise.

I. Let us look for a moment at *the all-inclusiveness*

of the promise—" all things work together for good."
It is generally agreed that the " all things " has
special reference to trials and tribulations. Here
is one of the most remarkable claims ever made
for Christianity. Here is certainly the boldest
justification of God's ways to man. Let us observe
exactly what it says. Perhaps we shall best be
able to grasp its significance if we approach it along
the negative route. We see clearly that, as Christians, we are not promised an easy time in this
world. Our Lord Himself in His teaching told
the disciples that they should have tribulations
and trials and sufferings. And in the same way
St. Paul teaches that " unto us it is given on the
behalf of Christ not only to believe on him but
also to suffer for his name's sake." The Christian's
view of life and of the world is realistic, not romantic.
He does not avoid troubles and problems. Neither
does he try to minimise the seriousness and the
greatness of the troubles and the problems. There
are those who think that the business of any
ministry of comfort, and of consolation, is to try
to show that the trials and the afflictions are not
really as bad as they appear to be. There are
well-meaning people who always try to take up
that attitude and that line when they try to help
their friends. It is true, of course, that there may
be a tendency in all of us to exaggerate our difficulties and thereby to increase our problems ; and it
is surely right that that tendency should be checked
and controlled. But it is not only fatuous, but

also dishonest, to try to make light of what is actually serious trouble. To tell a man who is writhing in agony that the pain is not quite as bad as he thinks it is, is both insulting and annoying. The intention may be good, but the result will be not only not to help the man, but to add to his trials by producing an additional source of irritation ! That is not the method of the Gospel. It takes the facts as they are. It faces them honestly. It covets no cheap victory or success by belittling the problem.

In the same way, its message to us is not just to tell us to set our teeth, to " stick it," and to be courageous. There are many who confuse faith with courage, and who would depict the Christian as one who, in spite of everything, just decides and determines to hold his head erect, and to go forward come what may. Courage as a virtue has been highly extolled during the past years. And let us agree that there is something very noble in the picture that is drawn. It is manly, it is upright to refuse to grumble and complain, to maintain one's poise and equanimity in spite of everything, to go on to the end unbroken and unbent —there is something truly noble and heroic in it all. But yet it is, essentially, a pagan virtue which has nothing whatever to do with Christianity. St. Paul does not call upon these people merely to be courageous. His appeal is not merely that they should hold on, and hold out, in spite of everything. As we shall see, his whole emphasis is not upon what they are to do, but upon what God *has* done,

118

is doing and *is going* to do for them. They are to continue, not by setting their teeth in a spirit of courageous determination, but rather by " setting their affections on things above." Courage in its real essence, and if it is the only thing that sustains us, is really a confession of hopelessness. It is the attitude of the man who refuses to give in though all is hopeless. But the Christian is saved by hope, and lives by his hope.

Neither is the Christian message just some vague statement to the effect that God loves us, and that therefore, somehow, everything must work out right, at the end. For that means that a gap is left between the love of God and the condition in which we find ourselves. It is virtually to avoid the problem altogether, to turn our backs upon it, and to forget it, and to think of something else. To be morbidly pre-occupied with the problem is thoroughly bad ; and it is always good to dwell upon the love of God. But the Christian position is not one which oscillates between these two positions. For that is not a real solution. It is a dualism which fails to connect the love of God with the difficulty and the problem. Now the whole glory of the Gospel is that it faces the whole situation without shirking anything, and yet shows the way out. Some of the older versions bring out this feature in our text very clearly by adding the word " God," to " all things work together for good," i.e., that " God works all things together for good to them who love Him." And that is undoubtedly what the Apostle teaches. These trials, difficulties and tribulations are not to be ignored, neither are they without any explanation whatsoever ; God uses them, and employs them, and guides them in such a manner as to promote our good. There is therefore no irreconcilable opposition between belief in God and the difficulties and trials of life. God uses them to our advantage and employs them in order to bring His own great purposes to pass. " All things work together for good to them that love God, to them who are the called according to His purpose." That then, is the ultimate justification of God's ways, that is the ultimate answer to all our questions as to why God allows certain things to happen.

II. We have but time for a passing word on what we might call the *limitation to the promise.* " All things work together for good *to them that love God, to them who are the called according to His purpose.*" In the original this is emphasised by placing " to them that love God " at the commencement of the sentence. " We know that to them who love God all things work together for good." The promise is definitely limited. It is not universal as to the people included. As we have had occasion to point out repeatedly, the popular idea of the love of God is the very antithesis of this. He is regarded as promising to bless all in exactly the same way. That He does so in His providential dealings with mankind in general is true. But following that, there is a great fundamental division

120

and distinction everywhere in the Bible between the saved and the unsaved, between those who have entered into a covenant relationship with God in salvation through Jesus Christ, and those who have not, or, to use the words of our text, " those who are called " and those who have not been called. Salvation is the result of the operation of special grace, and there are special promises to those who have received this grace. The Gospel has but one word to speak to those who do not believe on the Lord Jesus Christ. It is to exhort them to repent and to believe. It holds out to them no special promises until they have done so. Indeed, it threatens them with doom and disaster. It does not tell them that " all things work together for good " for the reason that it tells them that they are " already damned." As we have seen in our first section, special promises and comforts and consolations are not to be obtained directly. They are the consequences and results of salvation, of believing on the only begotten Son of God. They are offered only to those " who love God." We must mark the word " love." It is not mere general assent to a number of statements about God, neither is it some sentimental feeling. The word used for " love " involves the idea of a love which is anxious to do the will of God and to serve God, a love which is anxious to glorify God, and to please Him in all things because He is God. There is something truly terrible and alarming in our text. It tests us to the very depths. It carries the definite implication, that for us to question, and to query, God and His actions with the slightest suspicion of arrogance, just means that we are outside the promise. Those who love God know that all things work together for good. That does not mean that, at times, they may not be in a genuine difficulty as to the precise explanation of what is happening. But their spirits are always healthy and sound, though their minds may be baffled. They do not cease to love God. By our questions we often proclaim what we are, and where we stand. The one vital question for us is, do we love God ? Without our being in that relationship to Him we cannot possibly understand His ways, and we are outside the scope of His gracious promises. The promises are all conditional, and before we allow ourselves even to raise the question of *His* faithfulness, we had better examine *ourselves* and make sure that we have observed the conditions.

III. But we must look at what I choose to call *the mechanism of the promise*—the way in which it works. The apostle says that " all things work together for good to them that love God, to them who are the called according to His purpose." He says that we " know " this, that it is something which is well known and acknowledged, something that to the Christian is self-evident. How is this so ? The answer is partly doctrinal and partly a matter of experience. The doctrinal answer is already commenced at the end of our text—" to them who are the called according to His purpose."

—and is continued right until the end of the chapter. We know that all things work together for good to believers, because their whole position is dependent upon God and His activity. Our salvation is God's work. Listen to the argument : " For whom He did foreknow, He also did predestinate to be conformed to the image of His Son, that he might be the first-born among many brethren. Moreover, whom He did predestinate, them He also called: and whom He called, them He also justified : and whom He justified, them He also glorified." There is nothing accidental, or fortuitous, or contingent about God's work. It is all planned and worked out from the beginning right until the end. In our experience it comes to us increasingly, but in the mind and purpose of God, it is all already perfect and entire. Nothing can frustrate it, and that is why St. Paul asks his definite question, " What shall we then say to these things ? If God be for us, who can be against us ? " But it is not merely a matter of such high doctrine. There is a fact which confirms and substantiates it all : " He that spared not His own Son but delivered Him up for us all, how shall He not with Him also freely give us all things ? " Is God, Who actually delivered up His only Son to that cruel death on Calvary's Cross for us and for our sins, likely to allow anything or anyone to stand between us and His ultimate purpose for us ? It is impossible. With reverence we say that God, having thus done the most impossible thing, must of necessity do all else. If God did that, for our salvation, He will surely do everything else that is necessary. And if the death of Christ, with all that is so true of it, is the final cause of our salvation, surely everything else that we may experience, however bitter and cruel, must work to the same great end. God turned sin's most desperate action into the means of our salvation, and whatever lesser suffering we may have to bear, as the result of the activity of sin and evil, will be turned to the same glorious end. If we believe that we are in God's will, if we know that He loves us, and if we love Him in return and as a consequence of His love, then we can be certain that all things, whatever they may be, are working together for our good.

But God be thanked, we can also answer the question with regard to the mechanism of this glorious promise in an experimental manner, from the realm of experience. That our text is true, is the universal testimony of all the saints whose histories are recorded both in the Bible and in the subsequent history of the Christian Church. The ways in which this promise works out are almost endless ; but the principle which is common to them all is the one which we have emphasised already, namely, that there is but one ultimate good—the knowledge of God and the salvation of our souls. Holding that in mind, we see that trials and tribulations, and difficulties and distresses, work out in the following ways :

(*a*) They awaken us to the fact of our over-dependence on earthly and human things. Quite unconsciously, oftentimes, we become affected by our surroundings, and our lives become less and less dependent upon God, and our interests become more and more worldly. The denial of earthly, and human, comforts and joys often awakens us to the realisation of this in a way that nothing else can do.

(*b*) They also remind us of the fleeting nature of our life here on earth. How easy it is to " settle down " in life in this world, and to live on the assumption that we are here for ever. We all tend to do so to such an extent that we forget " the glories which shall be revealed " and which, as we have shown, should be the frequent theme of our meditation. Anything which disturbs our sloth, and reminds us that we are but pilgrims here, therefore, stimulates us to " set our affections on things above."

(*c*) In the same way, great crises in life show us our weakness, our helplessness, and lack of power. St. Paul illustrates that in this very chapter in the matter of prayer. "We know not what we should pray for as we ought." In a time of peace and of ease we think that we can pray, that we know how to pray. We are assured and confident, and we feel that we are living the religious life as it should be lived. But when trials come they reveal to us how weak and how helpless we are.

(*d*) That, in turn, drives us to God, and makes us realise more than ever before our utter dependence upon Him. This is the experience of all Christians.

In our folly we imagine that we can live in our own strength and by our own power, and our prayers are often formal. But troubles make us fly to God, and cause us to wait upon Him. God says of Israel through Hosea, " In their affliction they will seek Me early." How true that is of all of us. To seek God is always good, and afflictions drive us to do so.

(e) But all this is mainly from our side. Looking at it from the other side, we can say that there is no school in which Christians have learned so much of the loving, tender care of God for His own, as the school of affliction. While all is well with us, in our self-satisfaction and self-contentment, we shut God out of our lives, we do not allow Him to reveal to us His solicitude for us even in the details of our lives. It is only when we are so troubled that we " know not what we should pray for as we ought " that we begin to realise that " the Spirit maketh intercession for us with groanings which cannot be uttered." And it is to those who were " in the depths " that the sense of the presence of God has been most real, and the realisation of His sustaining power most definite.

The widow of a German Moravian bishop told me, a few months ago, that the universal testimony of all the Christians in Germany who had suffered untold hardships on account of their faith was, in her experience, that they would have missed none of these things, that indeed they thanked God for them. By these things they had been awakened to a realisation of the poverty of their Christian lives and experiences ; by these things also they had had their eyes opened to " the wonders of His grace." That is but their modern way of expressing what the psalmist puts thus : " It is good for me that I have been afflicted ; that I might learn Thy statutes " (Psalm cxix. 71). It is but the re-echo also of St. Paul's reaction to the verdict : " My grace is sufficient for thee ; for My strength is made perfect in weakness," which led him to say, " most gladly therefore will I rather glory in my infirmities, that the power of Christ may rest upon me. Therefore I take pleasure in infirmities, in reproaches, in necessities, in persecutions, in distresses for Christ's sake : for when I am weak then am I strong " (2 Corinthians xii. 9, 10). Is that our experience ? If we but " love God " and submit ourselves to Him, it most certainly will be ; for again I would remind you, that " all things work together for good to *them that love God*, to *them* who are *the called according to His purpose.*"

Further titles from the Evangelical Press of Wales

Martyn Lloyd-Jones: The Man and His Books by Frederick & Elizabeth Catherwood. A fascinating personal account of 'the Doctor' by his daughter and son-in-law.

The Welsh Revival of 1904 by Eifion Evans. A thorough but very readable study of the 1904 Revival, with a foreword by D. Martyn Lloyd-Jones.

In the Shadow of Aran by Mari Jones; foreword by D. Martyn Lloyd-Jones. Popular stories from farm life in North Wales vividly illustrating spiritual truths.

The Lord Our Shepherd by J. Douglas MacMillan. The author's first-hand experience as a shepherd makes this moving study of Psalm 23 extra special.

Christian Family Matters edited by Ian Shaw; foreword by Sir Frederick Catherwood. Clear biblical guidelines by experienced contributors on marriage, parenthood, divorce, abortion and other issues that affect family life.

Christian Hymns edited by Paul E. G. Cook and Graham Harrison. A comprehensive selection of 901 hymns; music edition and a variety of words editions available.

Christian Hymn-writers by Elsie Houghton. A collection of brief biographies of some of the great hymn-writers.

A SERIES of booklets for the earnest seeker and the new Christian by Peter Jeffery, born out of the practical needs of the author's own pastoral work:

Seeking God—for the earnest seeker after faith.

All Things New—a help for those beginning the Christian life.

Walk Worthy—guidelines for those who have just started on the Christian life.

Firm Foundations (with Owen Milton). A two-month study course introducing new Christians to great chapters of the Bible.

Stand Firm—a young Christian's guide to the armour of God.